and I Will Make Thee
WHOLE

and I Will Make Thee
WHOLE

HELPING FAMILIES WITH MENTAL HEALTH CONCERNS

Mental Health Resource Foundation

This publication is made possible by donations from Steven Petersen and from Craig and Jacoy Kellerstrass. Craig and Jacoy's donation is dedicated on behalf of their son Cameron.

© 2005 Mental Health Resource Foundation

ISBN: 1-55517-782-4
e.1

Published by Cedar Fort, Inc.
www.cedarfort.com

Distributed by:
Mental Health Resource Foundation

Typeset by Natalie Roach
Cover design by Nicole Williams and Kristi McMullin
Cover design © 2005 by Lyle Mortimer

Printed in the United States of America
10 9 8 7 6 5 4 3 2 1

Printed on acid-free paper

Contents

ACKNOWLEDGMENTS

Special thanks to James O. Mason, Joe J. Christensen, Sandra Callister, Sheldon Callister, Bern Vetter, Debbie Blair, and many other Mental Health Resource Foundation volunteers who have donated many hours in preparing this book for publication.

Introduction

Rex D. Pinegar

Rex D. Pinegar holds a doctorate of education in educational psychology from the University of Southern California. He has served as chairman of Educational Psychology at Brigham Young University. For twenty-nine years he served as a member of the Quorum of the Seventy in The Church of Jesus Christ of Latter-day Saints. He is currently on emeritus status.

Numerous resources are available to those seeking information regarding mental illnesses. This readings resource book has been specifically prepared to help those who accept the reality that humankind is both spiritual and physical in makeup. It does not offer professional help or direction; instead, it offers accounts from persons who have dealt with the complex challenges of mental illness in their families. It approaches the problem of mental illness from the perspective of the family rather than from purely a medical platform.

The premise upon which these readings are presented is that the soul of each human being includes all parts of the personality—the part we call physical, which relates to inheritance of genetic factors from earthly parentage, and the part that relates directly to spiritual characteristics. Man has his origin with God. He is the offspring of deity who is then clothed with mortal flesh for the experiences of mortality. The physical body is subject to the imperfections associated with earth life. These imperfections can have profound effects on our spiritual well-being. Each person is born with the light of Christ, however, which provides sufficient perfection for the individual to discern between good and evil.

Each section of this book contains writings by members of The Church of Jesus Christ of Latter-day Saints who have experienced symptoms of the respective mental health topic or whose spouse or parent has suffered from the malady.

Purpose

Oftentimes those suffering from mental illness find themselves treated as strangers in their own family and community. Because their behavior seems (and may indeed be) strange, persons experiencing such illnesses may find themselves estranged from the "normal" patterns of family and community life. The purpose of this book is to educate the reader concerning characteristics of various mental illnesses as well as viewing mental illness in a personal way. Each chapter ends with the author's testimony of the gospel of Jesus Christ and the hope that can be gained from the teachings of Jesus Christ, even in the most serious cases of mental illness.

No One Is Immune

No one is immune from social and emotional concerns. Mental health problems exist around the entire world, affecting those of high station socially and economically, those with rich religious backgrounds and ties, and those who walk the "normal" paths of life. This book has authors from the East and West Coasts of the United States and England. The poignant experiences of President Harold B. Lee of The Church of Jesus Christ of Latter-day Saints and of Latter-day Saint celebrity Donny Osmond serve to remind us of the universality of the challenges associated with mental health concerns. The reader will likely find a close identity with those who have bravely provided their experiences.

The Importance of the Family

As with any other illness, mental illness affects more than the person specifically experiencing its symptoms. The entire family becomes involved when a member of the family has a mental illness. The family may reach beyond the immediate siblings and parents. Each person is part of several groups that might at various stages of the illness serve as part of the "family." In the Church, an entire ward "family" may be involved in the person's illness in a direct way. Beyond the Church into the community, we may find a school or other social organization that becomes directly involved in the effects of the illness as it is expressed in the behavior of the ill person.

Unlike some physical medical illnesses that may be readily recognized, mental illnesses often remains hidden from public view or detection and thus their sufferers fail to benefit from the understanding and help of the entire community. Often fear is a factor in the minds of family and community groups because the mental illness may be unpredictable in its means of expression or the illness may be manifested in socially unacceptable ways. It is hoped that through this book much of that fear may be overcome and an empathetic attitude created, both among those observing and those enduring the effects of the illness, whether directly or indirectly.

Conclusion

Effective treatment always includes love, understanding, hope, and patience on the part of all concerned. Even if you do not have active mental illness in your family or among your associates, this book may increase your understanding and thus your ability to assist those who experience such difficult maladies. You may become the one who assists another who is suffering from some type of mental illness. You too may come to recognize, after all is said and done and after all earthly resources have been exhausted, that only Jesus Christ can make us whole: "And it came to pass, as Peter passed throughout all quarters, he came down also to the saints which dwelt at Lydda. And there he found a certain man named Aeneas, which had kept his bed eight years, and was sick of the palsy. And Peter said unto him, Aeneas, Jesus Christ maketh thee whole: arise, and make thy bed. And he arose immediately" (Acts 9:32–34).

Mental Illness

Dr. Rick H

Dr. Rick H is a psychologist who has worked in the mental health field for more than twenty-five years. He and his wife, Karla, have three daughters. He is a volunteer for the Mental Health Resource Foundation.

Most of us don't realize how widespread mental illness is or how much suffering results. Someone suffering from a mental illness can be found in each of our congregations and often among our own families. Occupation, social economic status, Church service, or obedience to the commandments does not guarantee anyone that life will be free from physical or mental illness.

Through the ages, mental illness has been among the most devastating and feared diseases of humanity. Today, thanks to ambitious and productive research, we have a better understanding of the causes of mental illness, and highly effective treatments exist. As a result, thousands suffering from depression, bipolar illness, schizophrenia, anxiety disorders, and eating disorders lead fulfilling and productive lives. Yet many still continue to live without recognizing their illness and therefore go without proper care. More than 54 million Americans have a mental disorder at any given time, although fewer than eight million seek treatment. One in five children has a diagnosable mental, emotional, or behavioral disorder; as many as one in ten may suffer from a serious mental illness. Seventy percent of afflicted children, however, do not receive mental health services (U.S. Department of Health and Human

Services, *Mental Health: A Report of the Surgeon General—Executive Summary* [Rockville, Md.: U.S. Department of Health and Human Services, Substance Abuse and Mental Health Services Administration, Center for Mental Health Services, National Institutes of Health, National Institute of Mental Health, 1999]). Late-life depression affects about six million adults, but only 10 percent receive treatment ("Factsheet: Mental Illness and the Family" [Alexandria, Va.: National Mental Health Association, 1998]). Some individuals suffering from mental illness are not able to live a "normal" life, even with proper mental health care. However, everyone with a mental illness can be helped in someway. We can help them by learning about mental illness and its symptoms, and how mental illness adversely affects family members.

Learning about Mental Illness

Mental illness "is an illness that affects or is manifested in a person's brain. It may impact on the way a person thinks, behaves, and interacts with other people. . . . Mental illnesses are real illnesses—as real as heart disease and cancer" (American Psychiatric Association, "What Is Mental Illness?" 2003). Mental and physical illnesses are much alike: "Mental illnesses are not the result of personal weakness, lack of character, or poor upbringing" (National Alliance for the Mentally Ill, "About Mental Illness," 2003). The term "mental illness" actually encompasses a number of disorders, and just like diseases that affect other parts of the body, they can vary in severity. People suffering from mental illness may not appear ill or look like something is wrong, whereas others may be confused, agitated, or withdrawn. The terms *mental disorder, psychological disorder, psychiatric disorder,* or *brain disorder* are used interchangeably with *mental illness.* Mental illness isn't a flaw in character; it's a flaw in brain chemistry.

Some of the more commonly known mental illnesses are the following:

- Depression

- Anxiety disorders

- Schizophrenia

- Bipolar disorder (also known as manic depression)

- Obsessive-compulsive disorder

- Eating disorders

These mental illnesses are usually chronic, and recovery often means not a cure but rather reaching the highest level of functioning possible for a given individual. Many, with proper interventions, can lead normal and productive lives. As is often the case with chronic physical diseases, however, recovery from mental illness is not always complete. Even with the best help, some are not cured. Recovery is relative and individual. For one, it may mean being able to stop medication and counseling without a relapse. For another, recovery may require taking one or more medications, attending regular counseling, and wrestling with ongoing symptoms—for a lifetime.

Dimensions of Mental Illness

Understanding the different dimensions of mental illness and how they affect the family are useful. Normal emotions will be discussed in the next chapter. Mental illness affects four areas of life: biological/physical, psychological/emotional, social/occupational, and spiritual/religious. These four dimensions are interdependent. Recovery occurs best when all four dimensions are addressed.

Biological/Physical

The medical aspects of mental illness include the biological/physical dimension. Knowing something about symptoms and diagnosis as well as medication and medication side effects can be useful in helping a person with mental illness. It is easy to forget that our brain, like all other organs of the body, is vulnerable to disease. Mental illness results from anatomical, physiological, or chemical abnormalities of the brain. The chemical processes in the brain of a person with a major depressive disorder are different from those of a nondepressed person. Specific medications can be used in combination with counseling to treat a mental illness. Brain abnormalities may be activated or made worse by stressful experiences or abuse of such substances as alcohol or drugs.

Symptoms and diagnosis. Mental health professionals communicate with one another and to the patient using the terms *symptoms* and *diagnosis.* For example, schizophrenia, major depression, bipolar disorder, panic disorder, and obsessive-compulsive disorder are diagnoses. A diagnosis is made by identifying the principal symptoms presented by the patient. Symptoms such as thoughts of suicide or death, sleeping too much or too little, loss of pleasure and interest, and loss of energy are characteristic of the diagnosis of major depressive disorder.

Medications and their side effects. Medications play a critical role in treating serious mental illness. Mental health medications can only be prescribed by a trained and licensed professional. Whether an individual uses medication is a decision that should be made by the prescriber and the person with mental illness, just as in taking a medication for any other medical problem. All medications have side effects. The continuing, uninterrupted use of medications by a person with mental illness may be as essential as is taking insulin on a regular basis by a diabetic. Stopping medication is a decision to be made only by caregiver and patient together.

Psychological/Emotional

Choosing the right counselor to help in developing personal coping skills is one psychological/emotional dimension of mental illness. Wounds need healing after a person accepts the reality of mental illness. The shattered dreams often associated with mental illness are repaired by improved coping skills. Counseling hastens this part of recovery. Obtaining appropriate professional help for a mental illness is not contrary to Latter-day Saint religious beliefs any more than is seeking professional help for another kind of illness or injury.

Counseling. Counseling is an essential part of recovery from serious mental illness. Those experiencing mental illness typically have negative and abnormal emotions and feelings. Treatment by a mental health professional assists in making the diagnosis and establishing goals by which progress can be achieved. The professional competence of the health-care provider is the single most important criterion in selecting a mental health caregiver.

Personal coping. Individuals with mental illnesses should strive to be more self-reliant. The capacity for self-reliance will vary from person to person. Individuals are as responsible as their mental illness will allow. Learning self-care skills and coping strategies and handling side effects of medications are only a few of the personal challenges that each person and each family member faces.

Social/Occupational

Family, community, and occupation are the social/occupational dimension of mental illness. Isolation and withdrawal are often components of mental illness. Negative stereotypes, stigmas, and misconceptions by friends, neighbors and co-workers are part of the challenge of having a mental illness. This challenge can extend through all areas of life for the patients and their families. Unfortunately, this maltreatment may also come from family members. Successful recovery requires maintaining social ties and engaging in some form of productive activity.

Maintaining social ties. It's hard to return to church meetings or other community settings after having been hospitalized for a mental illness. It can be difficult to find answers to what before seemed to be an easy question, such as "So, how are things going?" It is not easy to talk to those around you about something as private and painful as mental illness, but maintaining social ties is critical.

Productive activity. A person's self-esteem is closely related to participating in some form of productive activity. Regular employment can be maintained by many suffering from mental illness. For some, however, the disability is so severe that outside assistance is necessary. Regardless, the person with mental illness must find some place to make a meaningful contribution, no matter how trivial the task. History has shown that individuals with mental illness can make significant contributions to society. Abraham Lincoln, the sixteenth president of the United States, suffered from severe and incapacitating depression that occasionally led to thoughts of suicide (Carl Sandburg, *Abraham Lincoln: The Prairie*

Years and the War Years [New York: Harcourt Inc., 1954]). Ludwig van Beethoven, the brilliant composer, experienced bipolar disorder (D. Jablow Hershman and Julian Lieb, *The Key to Genius: Manic Depression and the Creative Life* [Amherst, N.Y.: Prometheus Books, 1988]). Many other examples exist of others with mental illness who have enriched our lives.

Spiritual/Religious

Maintaining a relationship with God is the spiritual/religious dimension of mental illness. Finding faith in a better tomorrow and acknowledging God as a loving being brings strength and comfort to those with mental illness. For some, maintaining faith in a higher power can be difficult, and family and church leaders play a vital role in their doing so. Faith in a loving Heavenly Father and His plan for us can bring peace, even when there is no obvious progress in the medical, psychological, or social dimensions of mental illness.

Hope and reassurance. Church leaders and families can help by providing hope and reassurance to those with mental illness. Each individual, regardless of how serious the condition, is a child of God and has the capacity to reach a higher level of well-being. Without hope, of what value is the future? Without hope, what meaning does sacrifice have? Without hope, how can anyone survive the challenges of mental illness?

Spiritual strength. Individuals coping with mental illness must maintain their inner spiritual foundation. We are spiritual beings first. The reassurance that God has a perfect love for each of us is essential. In *Valley of Sorrow: A Layman's Guide to Understanding Mental Illness,* Alexander Morrison writes concerning the importance of our Savior:

> My intentions in writing this book are neither clinical nor scientific in nature. They go beyond signs and symptoms, diagnosis and treatment, to my wish to apply a healing balm of Gilead to the scarified, suffering souls afflicted with mental illness and to those who love them. My desire is to ease their burdens and lighten the loads that gall and weaken them; to help them to reach toward God and have

hope and faith in Him and His purposes. . . . I pray they may bear their afflictions with hope for the future and with the knowledge that God has not abandoned them. His love, I know, is ever present and never failing . . . There will be times when the love of God is all that sustains those who bear the heavy burden of affliction and languish in the dark pit of despair. But I know from experience that His love never fails. It will see us through, though we walk in the valley of the shadow of death itself (see Psalm 23). (xviii)

Understanding the four dimensions of mental illness assures us that this kind of illness is more than just an abnormal brain chemistry. It's more than just seeing the doctor and taking medication. It's more than just knowing that God loves you and having faith you'll recover. For a balanced attack against such a powerful enemy as mental illness, "getting better" requires attention to each of the four essential dimensions.

Mental illness and the family. In dealing with severe cases of mental illness, the family goes through predictable stages. First, a *crisis* occurs. The person with mental illness behaves in such a way that draws attention. Maybe the individual threatens suicide, behaves so violently that the police must be called, or demonstrates some other strange behavior. As a result, the family feels overwhelmed, confused, or lost. They have no idea how to deal with the behavior or its cause. *Denial* often follows. Denial of the existence of mental illness in a loved one is common. It is a way of protecting oneself against the painful truth. The family wants to believe this is not really happening. It can't be mental illness! Nonetheless, the person with the mental illness continues to create additional crises, regardless of the home remedies used.

The family can no longer deny they have a serious problem in their home. They move from denial to *blaming* the person with mental illness. They may say to the person, "Snap out of it" or "Just try harder." Family members may begin to blame themselves. They may believe they could cure the illness if they could only "be more spiritual" or "be a better parent or spouse."

The *realization* finally sets in that someone they love has a serious problem. The family may still not understand what is going on or have any idea it is a mental illness. They realize that something tragic has occurred, everything they have tried has failed, and their lives are changed. The power of ignorance and fear of how others might react can result in years of delay before the family seeks outside help. The mental illness continues, and the roller-coaster ride of emotions by that time will have progressed to a chaotic level. The confusion of anger, guilt, and resentment may lead to a spiritual crisis. The love of God and His purposes may be questioned.

Many families however, do not go through such significant chaos when a family member has mental illness. These families never call the police, go to a psychiatric hospital, or deal with life-threatening behavior, but they struggle to a lesser extent with denial, blame, and anger.

Some families live their whole lives without getting help, without ever realizing a brain disorder is to blame, not themselves! They struggle and seem to cope, making the best they can of what sometimes is a terrifying nightmare. How could they know what no one has ever told them? Where would they have learned about mental illness? About medications? About recovery? Most families don't know anything about mental illness. Therefore, they simply wait and hope for the magic cure or give in to despair and give up!

Fortunately, more and more families are learning about mental illness and seeking help. It can take a long time for a family to reach the stage of *acceptance and understanding*. But how comforting it is to realize that there are others, many others—doctors, lawyers, church leaders, movie stars, and the list goes on and on—who have a mental illness. The following stories illustrate that no one is immune to mental illness. Finally, there are some answers. It is in this stage that the patient and the patient's family *learn to cope* by using medical, psychological, social, and spiritual resources.

Getting Help for Mental Illness

Dr. Rick H

Most of the challenges associated in dealing with mental illness can be attributed to two factors. The first is not understanding that mental illness is a disease. The second is telling the difference between mental illness and normal emotion. These two dynamics, more than any others, interfere with our understanding of mental illness and those suffering from its effects.

What Is Normal?

Normal emotions are feelings we all experience in everyday life. Sadness, for example, results from *common life events* such as the death of a loved one; *tragic life events* such as a divorce; or a *consequence of personal actions* such as guilt associated with sin. Sadness is a normal and expected reaction for such situations. In similar ways such other emotions as love, happiness, fear, sorrow, confusion, loneliness, and anxiety are normally experienced by any one of us given a particular life event or personal circumstance. Normal emotions are usually perceived as either positive or negative.

Another way to identify normal emotions is by asking, "What would other people experience given these circumstances?" If we are experiencing an emotion in a way similar to others, then what we are experiencing is likely normal and not part of mental illness. When the symptoms are more intense, however, or last longer, or are unusual and atypical, then mental illness is more likely. Furthermore, if a Church leader or family member has repeatedly attempted to assist the person with no progress, mental illness should be considered. A chronic, ongoing need for emotional support from others goes beyond what is normal.

Painful normal emotions, as distinct from mental illnesses, can be the result of negative childhood experiences or poor choices or behavior. Furthermore, persons with normal emotions can, on their own, use such interventions as willpower, positive thinking, and stress management techniques. Painful normal emotions are not medical conditions, and they respond to personal and family efforts.

Normal emotions are not mental illnesses and therefore can best be dealt with by using personal and family resources, including help from a religious leader or friend. In this case the preferred intervention strategies may include endurance, patience, increased spirituality, and learning new coping styles. Professional mental health practitioners have the saying, "We can't cure normal!" This saying reflects the belief that normal negative emotions may be necessary for healthy growing experiences and time and perseverance are the best treatment. In fact, using medication to deal with painful normal emotions should be avoided.

Elder Boyd K. Packer appears to be talking about the acceptance of normal emotions as part of our daily lives when he says:

> It was meant to be that life would be a challenge. To suffer some anxiety, some depression, some disappointment, even some failure is *normal*. Teach our members that if they have a good, miserable day once in a while, or several in a row, to stand steady and face them. Things will straighten out. There is great purpose in our struggle in life. ("Solving Emotional Problems in the Lord's Own Way," *Ensign,* May 1978, 91; emphasis added)

As Latter-day Saints, we are proud of our pioneer spirit to endure and to be victorious over significant life challenges! It's part of our heritage. Having "a good, miserable day once in a while" is not a mental illness. To deal with troubling normal emotions by going immediately to counseling can prevent character-building experiences. We don't go see the doctor for every bruise! But having a mental illness and failing to seek appropriate professional care is unwise, just as it is unwise to refrain from seeking appropriate medical care for diabetes or a broken arm.

Sin and Mental Illness

Mental illness is not necessarily connected with sin any more than cancer is! To an untrained eye the emotional turmoil experienced by a person with a depressive disorder or obsessive-compulsive disorder may seem similar to the turmoil experienced by a person carrying the burden of sin and associated guilt. But they are not the same, and they require different interventions. Guilt is a normal emotion associated with sinful behavior, which requires repentance and frequently confession to the appropriate Church leader. The feelings of sorrow and remorse normally experienced with guilt should not be confused with mental illness. In contrast, the overwhelming feelings of sorrow and remorse exhibited by a person with an obsessive-compulsive disorder typically do not represent reality. It usually becomes apparent to the Church leader that although persons with such a disorder have feelings of unworthiness, their perceived negative behavior is not equal to the magnitude of their guilt and sorrow. Those with mental illness should receive reassurance and support from family and church leaders and be referred to appropriate professional help. Real sin, if present, can better be treated by the Church leader *after* the person with mental illness has recovered sufficiently to recognize the difference between real and perceived sin.

Mental illness is not a punishment from God. We should not assume that mental illness is a result of sin. When Christ's disciples saw a blind man, they asked, "Master, who did sin, this man, or his parents, that he was born blind?" The Lord responded from a completely different perspective, giving a new concept of "no-fault" suffering. Jesus answered, "Neither hath this man sinned, nor his parents" (John 9:2–3). The idea that a mental illness comes as a result of God's punishment is not accurate. It is destructive to suggest that mental illness has been caused by someone's sinful behavior. But as noted, the cognitive dissonance resulting from guilt, unresolved sin, and persistent wrong behavior certainly takes a toll on one's state of mind. Alma the Younger, after all, was "racked with eternal torment," and Zeezrom's mind "was exceedingly sore because of his iniquities" (Alma 36:12; 15:5). The *General Church Handbook of Instructions* instructs Latter-day Saint leaders: "Do not attempt to explain why the challenge of a disability has come to a family. Never suggest that a disability is a punishment from God" (Book 2 [Salt Lake City: The Church of Jesus Christ of Latter-day Saints, 1998], 312).

A Continuum

We have been talking about those having mental illness and those who do not, as if they were separate and distinct groups of people. At times they are not. Individuals suffering from a mental illness have times when they experience normal emotions! A person with mental illness can experience sadness, anger, loneliness, high energy levels, or some other emotional state as part of a normal life experience. Unlike the science used to diagnose such physical diseases as cancer and diabetes, mental health assessment does not yet allow professionals the same level of scientific objectivity. Scientifically based laboratory tests for mental illness do not currently exist. Experience and rational judgment play a significant role in recognizing the difference between normal emotions and mental illnesses. A blending occurs in the continuum of normal emotions and mental illness.

Normal Emotions   **Blending**   **Mental Illness**

In the accompanying illustration, on the left side of the continuum are the negative and positive *normal emotions.* On the right side of the continuum are abnormal emotions, which are characterized as *mental illness.* Along the continuum are combinations of normal emotions and mental illness. From left to right, the condition becomes more intense and disabling.

At times it may be unclear whether someone actually has a mental illness. This gray zone in mental illness is no different from the zone of uncertainty found in other areas of medicine. Ten years ago a serum cholesterol level of 200 was considered normal. Today, this same number alarms some physicians and may lead them to prescribe treatment. Perhaps every adult in the United States has some degree of arteriosclerosis, but at what point on the continuum does normal move into the realm of illness? For even the best mental health professional, separating normal emotion from mental illness at times can be challenging.

Multiple diagnoses. Diagnosing mental illness can be further complicated because often an individual exhibits symptoms of several types of mental illnesses. We might like to think that the diagnosis of anxiety is absolutely different from a diagnosis of depression. Or that someone with bipolar disorder is unlike someone who has depression. This is not true. The symptoms of one mental illness often blend with the symptoms of another. Sometimes the symptoms of two or more mental illnesses occur with the same individual at the same time. Many of the individuals in the following stories have more than one mental illness.

Telling the difference. The process of telling the difference between a normal painful emotion and mental illness is referred to as making a diagnosis. The thresholds used to make those distinctions are best left to a mental health professional.

BIPOLAR AND RELATED DISORDERS

There is only one common type of bipolar disorder. Within this type there are variations in the episodes of depression and mania. Bipolar disorder causes dramatic mood swings from overly "high" and/or irritable to sad and hopeless and then back again, often with periods of normal mood in between. Severe changes in energy and behavior go along with these changes in mood. The periods of highs and lows are called, respectively, episodes of mania and depression.

Symptoms of both mania and depression are typically experienced in bipolar disorders.

Symptoms of Mania

The symptoms of mania, which can last up to three months if untreated, include the following:

- Extreme "high" or euphoric feelings—a person may feel "on top of the world" and nothing, even bad news or tragic events, can change this "happiness."

- Excessive energy, activity, restlessness, racing thoughts, and rapid talking.

- Unusual irritation or distraction.

- Decreased need for sleep—an individual may go for days with little or no sleep without feeling tired.

- Unrealistic beliefs in one's ability and powers—a person may have feelings of exaggerated confidence or unwarranted optimism. This can lead to overambitious work plans and the belief that nothing can stop the individual from accomplishing any task.

- Uncharacteristically poor judgment—a person may make poor decisions that lead to unrealistic involvement in activities, meetings and deadlines, reckless driving, spending sprees, and foolish business ventures.

- Sustained behavior that is different from usual—a person may dress or act differently from the way he or she usually does, collect various items, become indifferent to personal grooming, become obsessed with writing, or experience delusions.

- Abuse of drugs, particularly cocaine, alcohol or sleeping medications.

- Provocative or intrusive behavior—a person may become enraged or paranoid if his or her grand ideas are stopped or excessive social plans meet with disapproval.

Symptoms of Depression

- Persistent sad, anxious, or "empty" mood.

- Sleeping too much or too little; waking in the middle of the night or very early morning.

- Reduced appetite and weight loss, or increased appetite and weight gain.

- Loss of pleasure and interest in activities once enjoyed, including sex.

- Restlessness, irritability.

- Persistent physical symptoms that do not respond to treatment (such as chronic pain or digestive disorders).

- Difficulty concentrating, remembering, or making decisions.

- Fatigue or loss of energy.

- Feelings of guilt, hopelessness, or worthlessness.

- Thoughts of suicide or death.

- People with bipolar disorder often experience periods of normal mood and behavior following a manic phase; however, the depressive phase will eventually appear.

My Experience with "Mental Illness"

Dave Warren

Dave Warren is a connections education coordinator for the National Alliance for the Mentally Ill (NAMI). He is the divorced father of four children. He has been diagnosed with bipolar disorder, petit mal seizures, and obsessive personality disorder.

My experience with mental illness came about while I was serving my mission in South Korea. I was due to come home in March. Instead, I returned home three months earlier, in December. I was manic when I arrived. I was flying a little bit higher than the plane when I returned. I thought I was going to Church headquarters to discuss matters particular to South Korea with the General Authorities because I felt that I had some special insight into the needs of the Church in Korea. Instead, I found myself in Utah Valley Regional Hospital, where I remained for approximately one month. That is how long it took for the doctors to not only find a medication that worked for me but also for me to become stable on this medication.

For quite some time in the hospital I was defiant. I did not feel I needed to be in there. One of the college classes I had taken was sociology of mental illness. I felt I knew enough about mental illness to know that I was not mentally ill and that I did not belong in the hospital. In fact, on one occasion, a fellow patient and I attempted to break out of the hospital by throwing a small dresser through a window. We quickly found out how strong Plexiglas is.

It was a blow for me to have manic depression, known today as bipolar disorder (I prefer the term "biological brain disorder" better). Fortunately, medications worked pretty well. Following my discharge from the hospital, I finished the remainder of my mission in the Salt Lake City Mission. Upon my release my mission president encouraged me to not forget the time I spent serving in this mission. As I recall, he encouraged me to let it be known that I had served part of my two years in the Salt Lake City Mission.

When I returned home to Southern California I attempted to quickly adjust to life after the mission. However, for the most part I did not mention to people my missionary experience in the Salt Lake City Mission. I was aware of and sensitive to the questions that would arise if I brought it up. I felt I would be opening a can of worms. My main concern was that I did not want to be judged for having a condition with my brain. I was selective as to whom I told about my condition. My family, at least my parents and older brother, knew my situation. My younger three brothers knew something had happened to me, but they were not quite sure what. Some close friends knew of my condition, but for the most part I tried to keep a lid on the subject.

I chose to just get on with my life. During that time I finished my two-year degree and found and married my wife, Anne. It concerned me to tell my future wife that I had a mental illness. But I told her. After our marriage we moved to Utah. I went on to school. A couple of years into our marriage our first child, Jessica, was born. While in Utah I worked full time and went to school at the University of Utah. There I eventually completed my bachelor's degree in 1998. It was after completing my college education that my family and I had a series of life-changing events.

Those events began after my father shared a spiritual experience that had taken place in our home ward in Southern California. As an electrician, my father is often engaged in physical work, and he injured his shoulder at work. When he went to the ward library the following Sunday, he met a co-worker, who noticed that my father had injured his shoulder. Out of love and concern, this brother offered to give my father a blessing. My father responded that he had two sons at home who held the priesthood and could give him a blessing. This brother persisted, however, and stated that he desired to give my father a blessing. My father consented. This individual then gave my father a blessing in the library. My father told me that his shoulder was immediately healed. This was not all; my father related that he had never felt such an outpouring of love from the Spirit in his entire life. I later learned that this brother had blessed the lives of other people in the ward and had healed them through the priesthood as well. My father informed me that without a doubt this person had a gift to heal people.

At the time my father told me of his blessing, in addition to my mental challenges, I was battling with a neck injury that inhibited my ability to exercise. This was a source of great discouragement for me. I felt that I could deal with either the mental challenges or the physical challenge, but I was having a difficult time managing both. I decided to talk to my father about meeting this individual to receive a blessing.

The next time my parents visited us in Utah, I proposed my idea to my father. I was comforted by my father's response. He and this individual had become close friends, and he felt comfortable in arranging a meeting for us during our next vacation to California.

Finally, the time came for me to go with my father to meet this brother. At the stake center, I talked with him for a while and then received a blessing from him. I interpreted the blessing to mean that all would be fine. My neck felt good, and my mind seemed clear. I recall that this brother told me not to stop taking my medication all at once; however, I was confident that everything would be okay and I wouldn't need medication anymore.

In an effort to be cautious about tapering off my medication, I made an appointment with my general practitioner, who was prescribing my medication. I reminded the doctor that I had been on lithium for nine years without any problems and I was interested in stopping my medication to see if I really did need it. Because I had received a blessing, I did not fear stopping the medication. I had faith that everything would be okay. The doctor agreed to help me stop. The test of my faith began.

Approximately two weeks after I had been off my medication, I stopped sleeping and began to manifest other signs of mania. Not only was I not sleeping but I was keeping my wife and daughter from sleeping. To make a long story short, I was driving my wife crazy with my endless energy. My poor wife reached out to my father in California for help. He sensed the seriousness of the situation and the stress I was placing upon my wife and household. Consequently, he returned to Utah to see what he could do to help. The plan was to check me into a hotel and slowly get me back on lithium. We later found out how dangerous this plan was. Fortunately, this plan never was attempted. Instead, I ended up arguing with my father, asserting that he had the mental challenges and not I. My father proposed that we go to a hospital and let the doctors be the judge of the situation. I was so confident of my position that I readily agreed. I directed my father to LDS Hospital in Salt Lake City. It was there that I lost the argument. I remained locked up in the hospital, and my father was free to go.

This time I spent two and a half weeks in the hospital's mental health unit. As I slowly became stable on lithium again, I began to question how this whole situation had come about. I had received a blessing, and yet I felt it did not work. I asked my bishop why the blessing had not worked. Was I not worthy? I informed him that I felt I had sufficient faith. I shared with him the scripture in the Bible about a grain of mustard seed: "And Jesus said unto them, Because of your unbelief: for verily I say unto you, If ye have faith as a grain of mustard seed, ye shall say unto this mountain, Remove hence to yonder place; and it shall remove; and nothing shall be impossible unto you" (Matthew 17:20).

I understood the passage to mean that if a person had faith unto the size of a mustard seed, that person could move mountains. My bishop's response to me changed my life. He said: "All things are done according to the will of our Father in Heaven." He went on to say that I had sufficient faith, but the Lord had placed a mountain (bipolar illness) in my path and he did not want it removed by my faith. That was the key: "according to the will of the Lord." This response caused me to reflect on what had happened to me and to look at the big picture. I was now able to look at my situation in a completely different way.

I've relied a lot on my patriarchal blessing, which says that the veil was drawn so that I would fully understand the opportunity to understand the power of faith. It is an interesting statement. I don't think my faith was in vain in this experience of asking for a blessing and receiving it. If I had been completely healed by the blessing, I would likely have gone on with my life and never thought further about mental illness. As a result of the challenging experience of having mental illness, however, I have met people who have been a huge blessing in my life. I have learned to be more open with my situation. I now have an opportunity to work for the National Alliance for the Mentally Ill and interact with other persons who also experience biological brain disorders (mental illness) and their families. It has truly been rewarding for me to share what I have learned with others facing similar circumstances. I have the opportunity to interact with others who suffer from similar problems. I have learned that if I don't take my medication, I will probably find myself in the hospital again. I serve now as elders quorum president. I have four children. I say my prayers and I take my medication every day.

My patriarchal blessing also says that the blessings I will receive will be "many and great and varied." I guess having a mental illness could be considered one of those "great and varied" blessings. I know the Lord is mindful of me as an individual. I know it is through the Lord our Savior that we have the gospel. He has blessed me with a beautiful family. I know as I have looked back at my own suffering, he has been there for me. There have been many dark days when I had a lot of negative thoughts. But I know in looking back that the Lord has been there, and he has blessed me.

"Mommy"

Name Withheld

A stay-at-home mom, the author is married and has two children. She writes about what it was like to grow up with a mother who had bipolar disorder.

For twenty years I lived with a mentally ill mother. She is bipolar with schizophrenic tendencies, but we didn't know this until I was older, so growing up with my mom was rough. She was mean, both physically and emotionally. Some days she seemed depressed and would cry for long periods of time. Other days, she was angry. Her behavior was completely unpredictable. It was like walking on eggshells living in our home.

My mom was always worse when my dad was away at Church meetings, work, and other activities. When I was about eight years old, he left on a business trip, and things became really crazy. My sisters and I were playing downstairs, and my mom called us to come up. I don't remember all the details, but my mom got angry with me. I was still standing on the stairs when she grabbed me by the hair on my head, yanked me up the stairs, and threw me into the piano near the top of the stairs. It hurt, and I cried.

For several years while I was young, my dad served as a counselor in the bishopric (and later in the stake presidency). While he sat on the stand, we kids braved it out in the congregation with my mother. She had a lot of extreme religious beliefs. For example, we weren't allowed to watch TV, talk on the phone, or read the newspaper on Sunday. On occasion, we were also forced to fast before we were eight years old. When we were young, she didn't allow us to take the sacrament if she didn't feel we were well behaved. I felt like a bad child and was so embarrassed. It felt that the entire ward was watching and wondering why I wasn't worthy to take the sacrament. Religion and the concept of a loving God became confusing to me.

My mom frequently locked my two sisters and me out of the house. When she couldn't deal with us anymore, she would send us outside and lock all the doors so we couldn't get back in. The incident I remember best happened on August 13, 1975, while my mom was pregnant with my youngest sister. I was seven years old, and my other sisters were five and three. My mom was angry with us because we had played with the blinds in the bedroom, so she locked us all out of the house. This particular time, it seemed that we were locked out for a long time. Because I was the eldest, I always felt that I needed to take care of my younger sisters. I can still remember how awful I felt. I felt abandoned, like I was on my own and no one in the world loved me or cared about me. I sat in our front yard on the electrical box and cried. This sort of thing went on month after month, year after year.

As a child, I cried a lot. By the time I was a teenager, I refused to cry in front of anyone anymore. I only cried alone in my bedroom. I didn't want to give my mom the satisfaction of knowing she had hurt me again. She could hit me with a metal or wooden spoon all she wanted, but I learned not to cry a single tear. It always really hurt, and I felt terrible, but I did not cry.

Midway through the sixth grade, when I was eleven, I rebelled. It was during Christmas break. (My mom was especially bad during holidays). I was in the band at school, and so my parents bought me a flute for Christmas. The flute was expensive, and I knew that was all I would get, so I was surprised on Christmas morning when I received a stuffed animal and a backpack, too. My mom always thought we weren't appreciative enough and would take back part of our gifts. Sometimes we would get them back at a later time, sometimes we wouldn't.

That year, after one of my friends called to tell me what she got for Christmas, my mom really lost it. She called my friend's mom and chewed her out for letting her daughter call and tell me about her gifts. Needless to say, I didn't play with that friend anymore. Her parents didn't want her to hang out with me because it caused problems with my mom. That was the breaking point that started my official rebellion. I had to fight back somehow, and I chose the only way I knew.

When I returned to school in January, I received an award that I had been chosen to get before Christmas break. Some time later, my teachers told me that if the award had been based on my performance and grades after the break, I wouldn't have received it. They couldn't figure out what had happened. My grades dropped. I started to swear and purposefully be disrespectful. I didn't want to go to church. I just didn't care anymore.

I decided then that I would drink alcohol. I wanted to do the opposite of anything my mother wanted me to do.

My teenage years were really rough. My mom and I continued to clash, and she continued to beat me and tell me what a rotten kid I was. I drank a lot, went to lots of parties, and hung out with some bad friends—people I knew my mom wouldn't approve of. I'd sneak out of the house every weekend and stay out all night. I tried twice to commit suicide. I did lots of scary things. I was lost and had no where to turn for help. Alcohol was my only escape from my awful life.

I started to straighten out when I was seventeen. I quit partying and drinking. That was hard. I needed to drink to cope with my home life, which was a complete mess. Now I began living a facade. I didn't want my "normal" friends to know how weird and bizarre my mom really was, so I made up things. I pretended she was normal. I talked as if she was just an average mom. I never shared any real stories, and I didn't let anyone meet her or come to my house. When I went on dates, I met the boys at the corner, in my front yard, or right at the front door. I definitely didn't want them to meet my mom. Things were bad and definitely not normal, but I put on a front for the people around me. I still hurt inside, but it worked for a time.

When I was twenty, I met a good therapist. I started group therapy and counseling. It was so nice to talk to someone qualified, who understood what was going on and who told me that my mom was mentally ill. At first I was relieved to hear she was mentally ill because that explained her bizarre behavior over the years. Later I was angry. Especially with God. I couldn't understand how a kind and loving God could let me live in such awful circumstances with such a mean mom. It just didn't seem right. These were difficult feelings for me to work through.

Almost a year later, I married. It was so nice to move out and get away from my mom, but it was hard to return and see the rest of my family still suffering. I missed them and had a difficult time leaving them there with her. A year after I was married, my parents divorced—something I had prayed for since I was seven years old. After a psychological evaluation, the court awarded my dad custody of my six younger sisters and brothers. What a wonderful thing! My feelings and experiences had been validated by a court of law. My siblings would no longer have to go through the same experiences we had had in living with Mom.

After several years of counseling, I have found that the memories of growing up with a mentally ill mom are no longer overwhelming. My memories still aren't pleasant or happy, but I can deal with them. I still have a really hard time on Mother's Day, and I wish I could have a normal mom like other people do. I have children now, something that wasn't easy. I feared having children for many years because I worried I might turn out like my mom and didn't want to put anyone through an experience like that, but I love being a mom and a wife. I feel that I'm a good mom and wife, and I love my kids and husband a lot. I still remember (and will never forget) how hard it was living with my mom. That helps me to try to provide a better life for my children.

Some of my siblings still struggle with their memories of growing up with a mentally ill mom. It is hard to watch them suffer, knowing their lives could be better. I can cry sometimes now, wishing I had a mom I could talk to about my life and my children. My mother lives alone in a nearby city. We occasionally visit her. She typically doesn't open the door when we come, so we leave gifts at her door.

I've accepted that my mother has a serious mental illness. I've been able to forgive her, my dad, and even God for my childhood pain more and more as I grow older. I've learned about a different God and a different religion from the one I learned about in my home growing up. I started praying so I could tell God I was mad at him. Now I pray for many other reasons, though at times, it has been hard to believe that God would allow me to go through all that I've been through. It is not that I don't have a testimony. I do. I wouldn't go to church if I didn't think it was true. I have a temple recommend. I've been married in the temple. I want to be with my husband and children for eternity. I want to grow closer to God. I always want to be progressing.

I don't know why all of this happened. I doubt I will ever know all of the answers, at least not in this life.

When One Door Closes, Another Opens

Judy Cannon

Judy and her husband, Richard, are the parents of three adopted children and two foster children. One of their adopted children, who was diagnosed with bipolar disorder, committed suicide.

In May 1998, our second child, Nathan, called me from Utah State University to share a significant experience of the day. He recounted his moments on the internet in a bipolar chat room. After he had expressed some concerns in the chat room about his life, from somewhere in America came the following words, which sank into his sad, young heart: "When one door closes, another opens." This statement affected him deeply. It was a response that seemed to resonate hope. He spoke only briefly of this high-tech, yet highly personal, experience, but he wanted me to know that he had encountered something of value that day.

When doors close, when hard things happen, when life seemingly spares us no grief, what are we to do? Such times are critical junctures in life. What do we do with such experiences except grieve? When some doors close, we experience a painful separation. Likely, we hadn't known the door to be so massive in its weight that we couldn't alter its closure. Why couldn't the door be left ajar allowing us to have the opportunity to change the course of events? Loss of status, wealth, health, children, a spouse, even hopes and dreams often constitute a closing. Such losses pose difficult questions. They ask us to change. We begin that change when we ask the question, "What am I to learn from this experience?"

The Lord gives clear answer to that query: "Draw near unto me and I will draw near unto you; seek me diligently and ye shall find me; ask, and ye shall receive; knock, and it shall be opened unto you" (D&C 88:63). Asking not "Why me?" but "What is there to learn?" allows us to draw near to God. To find, to receive, to have the door opened are the blessings that come from asking the critical question, "Dear Lord, what would you have me learn?" We can all justify a bitter response to our trials, or we can look to this scripture as our guideline to the way the Lord has designed for us to move through this difficulty with success, to glean the lessons to be learned, to feel the love of the Savior, and to arrive at a new place in our lives through the new door he has so mercifully opened. Clearly, the underlying theme of this scripture is that the Lord waits for us to access his blessings. Let us access those blessings by asking, "What am I to learn?"

Doors That Have Closed

Perhaps the first door that closed for me was recognizing that I couldn't bear children. Accepting that reality was difficult, but adoption seemed reasonable and good. I would say it was a marvelous opportunity opened to Rich and me. With that godsend, however, I have been given some experiences that have been truly challenging. Three children whom I love have had severe problems.

Our second child, Nate, was loving, funny, and easy to deal with, and he grew in stature and faith. He worked hard in school and was very popular. Good looking and a great athlete (he excelled in diving), he had many friends and was a class officer.

He graduated from high school with honors and left for the Brigham Young University Jerusalem Study Abroad program soon after completing high school. While there, as he was preparing for his mission, he became so depressed that he had to be accompanied home by a caring fellow student. He had been unable even to pack his bags for the return trip. He had not eaten well for many weeks. When he returned to Salt Lake City, he was in a catatonic state of depression. We took him to a psychiatrist, and he was started on antidepressants.

For months Nate hid in his room and refused to see even his best friends. He would not participate in our family Christmas activities. He ate only if a McDonald's meal was taken down to his room and someone ate with him.

By April he was well enough to enroll in BYU extension courses. He started to work hard, but within a few weeks he began skipping classes and preferred to be having fun. He wanted only to ride his motorcycle. As he became more and more irresponsible, he became somewhat violent and had to be committed. In the hospital he acted normal and was released in three days. That night he vandalized our home. Eventually he was diagnosed with manic depression (also known as bipolar disorder) and given a different medication. We learned later that his irresponsibility, anger, and pursuit of pleasurable activities were manic behaviors related to his bipolar disorder. His mood seemed to stabilize on the new medication, but he became reserved and quite isolated.

The next spring Nate enrolled at Utah State University in Logan. He struggled with school but made it through a year and a half of college. With proper medication he seemed to be doing much better. This was a time of recovery. The family began to heal. Then in May 1998, on the Saturday we were planning to bring him home for the summer, we received a phone call. Nate had been found dead. He had taken his own life. This was shortly after the conversation I had with him on the phone about his new insight that "when one door closes, another opens."

As a result of this experience we have had some strong and difficult feelings to work through. For example, my husband is a physician, an endocrinologist, and has experienced feelings of guilt. He has felt that he should have understood mental illness better and should have been able to help our son. I'm convinced that one of the most painful trials an individual can have is for a loved one with mental illness to end his or her life by suicide. We learned that mental illness was not the temporary or transient social and emotional concern caused by the normal wear and tear of mortal life. Rather, it is the mood or thought disorder brought on by physical, chemical changes in the brain that impair a person's ability to cope with life's demands.

Life Is Officially Unfair

Through e-mail came this thought: "All reports are in—life is now officially unfair." I have felt this. Life is difficult. It would be a rare individual who is not burdened by life's twists and turns. Nevertheless, we all come to a critical point, likely a multitude of times, where we have to ask,

"What do I do with this experience? How can I handle this?"

I asked this question in a state of tremendous sorrow within minutes of learning of Nate's tragic death. What could I learn from something so horrid? Within an hour, an understanding came to me via the Comforter that I had no unfinished business with this son. What a remarkable insight! I had never considered fully until that moment, by far the saddest moment of our lives, that I had no regrets. I had done all a mother could do.

This was the beginning of many spiritual moments related to our son's life and death. It helped me take stock of the decision our family made, along with the extended family and even our neighborhood, to support this formerly glorious boy as he experienced the cruel twists of mental illness taking its toll. This choice was a difficult one for everyone, because those who suffer from the ravages of mental illness often have no redeeming qualities to their behavior. To choose to support rather than to reject is uncommon. Nate gave all of us an opportunity to understand the best we could that mental illness is not a character flaw or sign of moral weakness. As Moroni observed, "Ye receive no witness until after the trial" (Ether 12:6).

Initially my husband and I had a difficult time accepting the fact that Nate had died alone. Soon afterward a young man in our ward was diagnosed with brain cancer. After a valiant twenty-month battle, he died. The night he died, my husband and this young man's father had the privilege of ordaining him to the Melchizedek Priesthood. It was soon after his eighteenth birthday. At least fifteen friends spent the entire evening with this young man until he passed away in the early hours of the morning. He was a great young man and had support from friends, neighbors, and fellow Church members. I believe Nate too had a fatal brain disease, a bipolar disorder. But he died alone.

I experienced much anxiety as I considered the awful question of whether the Lord would accept Nate because of his deeds. The answer came through a friend, who reminded me that the Lord could have prompted someone to intervene. That the Lord allowed him to go home was the only conclusion we could come to. The next day, a Sunday, our wonderful stake president met with the priesthood and the Relief Society to speak on the subject of suicide. He asked that no one judge but rather lend support.

The comfort to me and to those whose loved ones die in this manner is reflected in the words of Elder Bruce R. McConkie:

> Persons subject to great stresses may lose control of themselves and become mentally clouded to the point that they are no longer accountable for their acts. Such are not to be condemned for taking their own lives. It should also be remembered that judgment is the Lord's; He knows the thoughts, intents, and abilities of men; and He in his infinite wisdom will make all things right in due course." (*Mormon Doctrine* [Salt Lake City: Bookcraft, 1966], 771)

The Weight of Hard Experiences

I have not loved these hard experiences. In fact, they have weighed upon me greatly, but I have valued them for myself and even for my family. President Spencer W. Kimball knew a good deal about suffering, disappointment, and circumstances beyond his control. He said:

"Being human, we would expel from our lives physical pain and mental anguish and assure ourselves of continual ease and comfort, but if we were to close the doors upon sorrow and distress, we might be excluding our greatest friends and benefactors. Suffering can make saints of people as they learn patience, long-suffering, and self-mastery. The sufferings of our Savior were part of his education" (*Faith Precedes the Miracle* [Salt Lake City: Deseret Book, 1972,] 98).

I relate to thoughts that President Howard W. Hunter shared during general conference in the fall of 1987. He said, "Doors close regularly in our lives, and some of those closings cause genuine pain and heartache. But I *do* believe that where one such door closes, another opens and perhaps more than one, with hope and blessings in other areas of our lives that we might not have discovered otherwise" ("The Opening and Closing of Doors," *Ensign*, November 1987, 59).

What Is to Be Learned?

What is to be learned from such an experience? Much—and it is good. I believe Nate is now wrapped in the loving arms of the Savior. After his death, our entire neighborhood seemed united and supportive. Each of us was asking, "What should I do to choose the better way?" What a blessing to experience what the Lord needed us to understand about some of His choice children here on earth.

These trying times, whatever they might be, bring into focus the essential elements of our relationship with Christ as our Savior. We pray as we have never prayed before, and those prayers are part of the process of being comforted and gaining understanding as doors open to our spirit, our soul, and our heart of what is to be learned from such experiences. I don't remember my prayers during the dark times, but I remember always knowing that God had a plan for Nate and for us. It was like a constant prayer, ever present in my mind and heart, feeling always that his plan would unfold to the benefit of all. Did He have in His plan that Nate would take his own life? I don't know. But did He have in His plan that Nate would feel His everlasting mercy? Of course! Did He have in His plan that Nate would feel His love and be folded into His arms, knowing that he was home and free of his afflictions and safe evermore? Yes! What an important recognition of the hand of the Lord in our individual lives.

Conclusion

I would not ask for different circumstances in my life. My testimony is that the Lord with all his tender mercies has never forsaken me. He has blessed me with a family, with trials never anticipated, and with an overwhelming sense of his love for me. From what would appear a life of many sorrows have come rich and remarkable blessings. There is great hope upon which all of us can draw. Our faith assures us that this is true.

As doors closed and losses came, the question "How can I benefit from this?" allowed me to draw near to the Lord and await what needed to be revealed. I do not begrudge the difficulties, for they have given me experiences only the Lord could foresee, experiences that would benefit me eternally, and they have been for my good. He designed a way for us to draw near unto him and for him to draw near unto us. It was through trials that even Joseph Smith had to learn (D&C 122). Why, then, not us?

DEPRESSION AND RELATED DISORDERS

There are generally two common types of depressive disorders. Within these types are variations in the number of symptoms, their severity, and persistence. *Major depression* is manifested by a combination of symptoms that interfere with the ability to work, study, sleep, eat, and enjoy activities once found pleasurable. Such a disabling episode of depression may occur only once in a lifetime, but more commonly such episodes occur several times. A less severe type of depression, *dysthymia,* involves long-term, chronic symptoms that do not disable but do keep a person from functioning well or from feeling good. Many people with dysthymia also experience major depressive episodes at some time in their lives.

IT'S
JUST
AS
REAL

Symptoms of Depression

- Persistent sad, anxious, or "empty" mood.

- Sleeping too much or too little, or waking in the middle of the night or very early morning.

- Reduced appetite and weight loss, or increased appetite and weight gain.

- Loss of pleasure and interest in activities once enjoyed, including sex.

- Restlessness, irritability.

- Persistent physical symptoms that do not respond to treatment (such as chronic pain or digestive disorders).

- Difficulty concentrating, remembering, or making decisions.

- Fatigue or loss of energy.

- Feelings of guilt, hopelessness, or worthlessness.

- Thoughts of suicide or death.

Death's Dark Angel Strikes

Brent L. Goates

President Harold B. Lee served as a member of the Quorum of the Twelve Apostles, president of the Quorum of the Twelve Apostles, first counselor to President Joseph Fielding Smith, and president of The Church of Jesus Christ of Latter-day Saints. He was married to Fern Lucinda Tanner for thirty-nine years. They had two children. This chapter identifies symptoms of depression displayed by President Lee as he experienced the normal process of bereavement following the death of his wife and of his eldest daughter, Maurine.

Elder Harold B. Lee was blessed greatly in July 1963 when he married Freda Joan Jensen, [but] here we concentrate on the necessity for Elder Lee to encounter heartbreaking sorrow once more. Coupled with his many triumphs, he was again brought low through personal tragedy.

This next trial commenced with an assignment to travel abroad in August 1965. In July, Elder Lee met with Elder Paul H. Dunn to plan for conferences in Samoa and Australia, a trip that was to last from August 21 until September 19, culminating with a new stake to be organized at Adelaide, in New South Wales, Australia.

Shortly before his departure, however, Elder and Sister Lee drove to Provo to see the Wilkins family; while there he gave Maurine a blessing for her forthcoming motherhood.

After only six days in Hawaii, Elder Lee was awakened at 5:45 A.M. on Friday, August 27, by a shocking telephone call from his wife giving him the shattering news that Maurine was in critical condition at the Utah Valley Hospital in Provo, Utah. Elder Lee immediately phoned the hospital where his son-in-law, Ernest J. Wilkins, told him through his sobs that the doctors were fighting for her life, but that they were giving him no hope. Elder Lee immediately obtained reservations for a flight back home. Minutes later, Ernie called again to say that Maurine was gone, dead at age thirty-nine from a lung embolus, while expecting her fifth child.

Elder Paul H. Dunn, then a newly called General Authority on his first lengthy trip with a senior Apostle, has vivid recollections of sharing this tumultuous event in the life of Elder Lee. He had witnessed Elder Lee giving encouragement and faith to the grieving family of a Hawaiian stake president just the day before. The deceased wife, Sister Moody, was a dear friend of Sister Fern Lee, and the counsel Elder Lee had imparted in his funeral address he would have to follow himself the very next day. Elder Dunn's memory of this experience follows:

> In sharing the traumatic experience of the sudden loss of one's cherished daughter in this way, I saw the tender, father side of President Harold B. Lee. We knelt in prayer, and while it was one of the most heart-tugging experiences I have ever had, it was also one of my most spiritual blessings. I learned from this experience how a man reacts who is really under fire with his apostolic calling. I saw there the making of a prophet; I saw how a man destined to be a prophet truly acts under pressure.
>
> I'm not implying that that's why his daughter died, but certainly the Lord permitted it to happen. President Lee was struck down by this blow, as any father would be at the loss of a loved one, a precious daughter. But to witness that even in that terrible moment the adversary still didn't have control, I thought, was one of the greatest lessons of my life.

Elder Lee's journal captures his immediate sorrow. He wrote: "My heart is broken as I contemplate the passing of my darling 'Sunshine' and the great need that Ernie and her family of four little ones have for her."

Elder Lee's plane was delayed forty-five minutes in leaving Honolulu, and to his already abundant worries came the additional concern that he might not make a tight connection at Los Angeles. Elder Lee called this plane trip "the longest and most tortuous ride I have ever taken. It seemed like an eternity."

At the end of the flight in Salt Lake City was awaiting the most sad and shattering scene of his life:

> I found all my little families at the airport. I was

completely overwhelmed and could hardly control myself physically or emotionally when I saw the little motherless family with Ernie. I went to our home to lay plans for the days ahead. All of us seemed to be in a daze from the shock and the strain of my darling Maurine's passing. This seemed to compound my sorrow in losing Fern three years ago next month.

Four years later Elder Lee preached about this never-to-be-forgotten scene, at a stake conference in the Brigham Young University Sixth Stake. At that time his recollection was:

Suddenly, and without warning, that little mother was snatched away in a moment. The pleadings of Grandfather over in the Hawaiian Islands and the piteous cries for the mercies of the Almighty to spare her were unavailing. And in the hospital, surrounded by doctors with all the medical skill that they could summon, she slipped away. The children were called, and around the lonely table in the family room they sat with bowed heads sobbing their hearts out. The grandfather was summoned to come and that night flew home, and all the family were at the plane to meet him, hoping that surely he could do something to lift the burden. And with arms surrounding that little family the grandfather said: "I do not know how you can be so brave. Grandfather is crying his heart out and you stand here with your arms around each other, seemingly with no tears." And one of them said: "Grandfather, we have no more tears to shed. We have cried our tears away all day long."

That drama was enacted right here in your community. I was the recipient of that phone call; I was the grandfather who pleaded at five o'clock in the morning, "Please, God, don't let her die." But it was as though our Heavenly Father was saying, "I have

other plans," and all the faith that could be mustered
was unavailing.

Life had to go on, and the shocked family in Provo needed loving
administration. Aunt Helen never left the family those first two weeks.
The bags she had packed for a two-week vacation, which was aborted
at the news of Maurine's death, served Helen well as she stayed to take
care of her sister's grief-stricken family. That first night she slept with
Maurine's daughter, twelve-year-old Marlee, to comfort her. This little
flaxen-haired girl had a dream so vivid that she awakened, gripped her
aunt by the arm, and said: "Aunt Helen, I've had such a funny dream!
I dreamed we were sitting in the family room with Mother—you and
me and Jane [her cousin]. Mother was sewing a button on Jay's shirt.
[Jay was her younger brother.] We were all talking while Mother sewed.
Jay came in and said he was sad because Mother was gone, and I said,
'No she's not gone—see, she's right here—can't you see her?' Jay couldn't
understand what I was saying, and I asked you and Jane if you could see
her, and you just smiled. None of you could see her, but I could—I knew
she was there. Isn't that funny, Aunt Helen?"

Aunt Helen, conditioned by the wise teachings received in her childhood home, replied: "No, Martsy dear, that's not just a funny dream. I
think it's Heavenly Father's way of letting you know that even though
your mommy has been taken from you, she can still be with you when
you need her. You won't always be able to see her as you did in your
dream, but she'll be close by and you'll feel her presence. Remember your
dream, Martsy, when you're sad and lonesome for her, and it will help to
make you feel better." Reassured, Marlee went back to sleep.

The passing of Maurine Lee Wilkins was not just a family tragedy.
It sent an entire community into grief. As her friends and acquaintances
gathered at the Berg Mortuary in Provo, Utah, visiting stretched beyond
the announced hours of 6 P.M. to 8 P.M., extending from 5:30 P.M. until
10:30 P.M. It was one of the most amazing expressions of genuine sorrow
ever displayed in the passing of a young LDS community leader, who
had been active in church, Parent-Teachers Association, politics, faculty
wives groups of Brigham Young University, and the Chamber of Com-
merce.

The funeral services were held at noon on August 30, 1965, in the

East Sharon Stake Center. Elder Lee recorded his impressions of the funeral in these words: "Elder Marion G. Romney's closing sermon was a masterpiece, full of faith and hope and sound of doctrine. He was right when he said 'the veil was very thin.' We brought Maurine to Salt Lake to be buried in our family plot, opposite her mother. This gave us much comfort."

Five days later the grieving Elder Lee began to feel some hope, yet he couldn't find full relief from his sorrow. He wrote: "Our heartbreaking experience in losing our darling Maurine seems to bear promise of binding our families together as we all seek to share in the heavy burdens of sorrow in our loss. Somehow I seem unable to shake off this latest shattering blow. Only God can help me!"

In mid-September 1965 Elder and Sister Lee took their heavy-hearted families to a cafeteria dinner, but the Church leader observed, "Ernie is still having a struggle with his emotions, as am I." When friends came to visit him, any recall of the harrowing events of Maurine's passing left Elder Lee upset, resulting in journal entries such as this: "My nerves were so disturbed that it took me until 1:30 A.M. before I could get to sleep." On September 28, 1965, he wrote: "It seems as though I was experiencing some reaction following the strains of the past months. I find it difficult to sleep."

During the October general conference of that year, Elder Lee was a speaker at the special missionary session on Friday night and the first speaker at the Sunday afternoon session. His subject related closely to his own experiences and feelings and severely taxed him. Of this he wrote: "I discovered this talk and the one on the subject of trials and tribulations were almost more than I could do." He had said to the capacity crowd in the Tabernacle: "As I advance in years, I begin to understand in some small measure how the Master must have felt [in the Garden of Gethsemane]. In the loneliness of a distant hotel room, 2,500 miles away, you too may one day cry out from the depths of your soul, as was my experience: 'O dear God, don't let her die! I need her; her family needs her.'"

As always, holidays and anniversaries brought back memories and were the hardest days to emotionally surmount. November 13, 1965, was such an uneasy day. It was the eve of Fern's birthday and their wedding anniversary. But when Elder Lee arrived home late that night from attending a conference in the Klamath Stake near Portland, Oregon, tired and emotionally weary, his daughter Helen had a beautiful letter waiting for him to lift him over his depression. Despite this comfort, it was after 2 a.m. before Elder Lee could quiet his nerves and fall asleep.

Christmas 1965 offered another such emotional hurdle. Helen visited her father in early December and shared her ideas for spending the holidays together in a different way than ever before. She felt this would help them all to feel less keenly the loss of both Fern and Maurine.

Accordingly, the entire Lee family spent two days before Christmas and the three days following in a comfortable cabin home owned by kind friends in Kamas, Utah. All went well with little outward evidence of sorrow and sad remembrances of past Christmases. When they came down from their mountain cabin retreat after the holidays, Elder Lee left immediately for a trip to New York City. Upon his return he again recorded that he "had a sleepless night, perhaps due to a combination of a heavy heart and travel weariness."

The grieving continued sporadically for another year or more as Elder Lee struggled to gain an emotional foothold and make a new life after the family deaths had registered their tremendous effect on him. On the first anniversary of Maurine's passing, with the memories of his losses poignantly on him, and analyzing the event one year later, he wrote this commentary in his journal: "This is the anniversary of Maurine's sudden passing while I was in Hawaii. . . . I returned home that night to the saddest experience of my life, as I saw her shocked little family, hoping that Grandfather's return would somehow lift them above their tragic loss. Somehow my emotions and nervous tensions seem to have been intensified as the memories of Fern and Maurine come back to me now."

Undoubtedly Maurine's unexpected death did produce the "saddest experience of [his] life." She was in her prime, her family needed her so desperately, and she had always produced a never-ending source of sunshine and happiness for all who knew her. Her passing compounded his grief in losing Fern.

With one-half of his small family of four now taken away from him, Elder Lee's challenge was to courageously overcome his profound grief, which undoubtedly strengthened him for his future role as the Church's prophet. Certainly it filled his heart with empathy for all other sufferers. His funeral sermons and generous efforts at comforting the grieving souls about him, always a personal strength, now reached new heights of inspiration, in part because he had become acquainted with the bitter depths of despair. This experience was forever afterward a key to his spiritual power and compassionate service, and he learned to more fully appreciate the lesson taught in Hebrews 5:8–9: "Though he were a Son, yet learned he obedience by the things which he suffered; and being made perfect, he became the author of eternal salvation unto all them that obey him." The refining formula used by a loving Heavenly Father to season and prepare his son, the Savior Jesus Christ, while in the flesh, was also being applied for producing a mighty prophet of the last dispensation, Harold B. Lee.

Taken from L. Brent Goates, *Harold B. Lee: Prophet and Seer* (Salt Lake City: Bookcraft, 1985), 341–63. Used by permission.

"Thee Lift Me and I'll Lift Thee"

Stephen Hales

Steven Hales and his wife, Sue, are the parents of three boys and two girls. They tell the story of their child who has suffered from depression.

Revealing one's innermost challenges requires a sacred trust in others. It is my prayer that when you scan through the experiences we share here, you can accept them as intended. It is our hope that if you are currently experiencing similar challenges with brain disorders, whether yourself or a loved one, you will take the message to heart. Please open your heart and allow yourself to be teachable on issues that are generally social taboos. Be honest with yourself. Please, respect the honesty necessary for our family to share with you.

Introduction

When first contacted to be involved in writing for this project my heart leaped upward with the hope of being able to share some of what we have experienced. Families and parents can become isolated and tortured if they have to face events related to mental illness without a simple knowledge. This thought that others live "alone" in their suffering or that a loved one suffers needlessly is true torture for me.

My wife and I were like deer in the headlights when we realized that we had no clue to what this disease of depression was about to entail for us. We wandered dismayed and dazed for many months, attempting to continue on with the rigors of daily life as we dealt alone with our son's chemical imbalance. Finally, friends in our ward suggested that we contact the National Alliance for the Mentally Ill regarding NAMI's Family-to-Family Education program. We did.

Our Son

It took some time for us to accept the idea that our son had a mental illness. He experienced depression and on occasion psychotic episodes. Parents may not be the first ones to admit their child has a serious brain disorder. It may be a schoolteacher, a boss at work, or a friend at the mall who observes the first signs. In our case it was our neighbors. Our son had his first experience with his disruptive thought patterns while at our neighbor's house. We were at a ward dinner party only a few blocks away. We had been in the kitchen most of the night. We noticed as we pulled into our street two police cars and an ambulance in the middle of the road. Our son was shackled by the feet and handcuffed. Four officers were on his back. This episode is not something I have often spoken of. The prospect of the judicial system getting the upper hand as we initially explored our son's illness was not a positive experience. We realized then that an in-depth evaluation and consequent action based on it were needed. Over the years I found one of the most difficult parts of my son's mental illness to deal with was the periods of psychosis. They are like attempting to help a sleeping child who is screaming and flailing about in a deep dream.

When his illness was at its worst, our son would spend hours, days, weeks, and seemingly months alone in his room, having few calls and few visitors. Such is the nature of depression. We learned that although isolation seemingly allowed him to avoid many stresses, in reality it only prolonged his suffering. He had some true friends who would occasionally stop and talk and who were honest enough to express real love. He opened up to them. They respected his expressions and continue to do so today. We love them for that. During this time it seemed that my wife and I were on the inside looking out. It was a form of overexposure for us to reach out to anyone at that time. His grandparents, brothers, sisters, a few close friends, and we as parents became his keepers during the worst periods of his mental illness.

As Parents

As parents we questioned our ability to deal with a child with a brain disorder. We wanted to search out the cause of the mental illness. We learned it was important not to fixate on the cause, and it was even more critical to act on the options. In our case, grief initially surrounded us and our other children. Our son, whose future had looked so promising, now seemed diminished at the realization that his talents would be overshadowed. He had lost jobs, lost friends, and lost educational opportunities. Feeling awkward, most individuals who had once been close stopped saying anything to us. One literally mourns the death of expectations and dreams once held for one's child when mental illness strikes.

Stress between my wife, Susan, and me grew exponentially along with the realization that mental illness had become part of our daily life and would remain with us throughout mortality. The result was that our marriage was faced with what I believe to be the most trying scenarios possible. Though we did not know exactly what to do, at various important junctures inklings, promptings, and inspiration were given to us. At times, I admit, it seemed that little light seeped back to us. The prayers, blessings, and fasting seemed to fall short of correcting the injustice of mental illness.

Susan and I have been there. We have huddled in the dark, in silence, listening to the sobbing of our son and each other in what seemed to be a hopeless cause. The feeling of a dark mist around us made the edge of life as we knew it even closer. At times the days seemed to creep by ever so slowly. We initially hesitated to say anything to anyone unless we knew that the person had directly experienced mental illness.

Many marriages do not survive when dealing with mental illness. This may be due to one partner's accepting the issue and the other not. One might become bitter, while the other seems okay with it or talks openly about it. In our case, our marriage benefited greatly from our experience. We eventually grew because it was our nature to pull together rather than be drawn apart by these new challenges. The challenges created by mental illness still continue today.

As a Mother

Susan talks about her perspective:

"When each of our five children was born, I remember my husband making sure he counted all ten fingers and toes. He was looking to outward appearances for signs of traditional birth defects. We were over-joyed at the prospect that all three sons and two daughters were whole and healthy. We had experienced the miracle of birth and renewal of life within the covenant.

"Little did either of us expect a silent disease was lingering as a result of genetic factors that would lead to chemically based disorders, such as anxiety, attention deficit disorder, and depression. To some it may seem cruel to reveal such private matters, but please understand that the ability to accept such conditions in others outside the family was to be preceded by our ability to truly accept it in our own beautiful children. Parents, spouses, and siblings cannot be of any assistance until they accept it and vow to do their part.

"My education is in early childhood development. That training, I feel very deeply, has made a vast difference in my ability to accept my son's limitations."

Our Ward Family

Let me start off by posing a tough question. Pause and ask yourself, "In our own religious culture, do we as a whole tend to reject those who have fallen and perhaps have acted in less than acceptable ways?" Only those who have walked in the shoes of one suffering a similar malady or who are tuned to the Holy Spirit may lift a soul being tested by depression or some other yet undiagnosed chemical imbalance.

When you think about it, the phrase "as good as it gets" is a real term in the lives of many individuals who deal with mental illness on a daily basis. Hearing others' comments, such as "Just buck up," "Deal with it," "Tough it out," or "Have faith," can send the message that you are uncaring at the very least and possibly that you are totally cruel. Therefore, being hasty in passing judgment or avoiding those who may have such challenges may be risky. At times the things ward members said and did seemed to affect our spiritual welfare, physical health, and emotional well-being. As a result of my experiences, I now demand from myself far more observation, listening, contemplation, and compassion in attempting to understand another's feelings and perceptions than I had ever previously imagined.

I am grateful for my challenges and experiences. I continue to learn on virtually a daily basis that offering solutions or advice to those who are mentally ill needs to be tempered. Discerning the proper needs of one living with any type of brain disorder is a continual process. The disease is never cured. Nor will the individual be able to live risk-free in this life. I believe, before we can help those dealing with depression of any type, that we must first make an effort to understand basic brain chemistry. Current medications and counseling techniques, in combination, are usually successful to assist persons suffering from mental illness.

We had witnessed friends in the past being forced to tough it out "by faith alone" due to the ever-present stigma and embarrassment of depression. This is tragic. In light of our Savior's example of protecting those judged in ignorance or harshly by others, I imagine that this unnecessary suffering must deeply trouble him. Consider the difficulty when he sees fellow Saints casting judgment or ignoring the issue, as portrayed by the parable of the good Samaritan.

A friend shared the following story of a quiet moment with a son who was suffering from a deep depression and suicidal thoughts. The friend pictured the Savior standing at the edge of the bed holding his son's hand. Lovingly my friend pointed out, if his son had required surgery, there would have been flowers and meals for days and well-wishers would have arrived with get-well cards. Yet during the worst of times with his son, my friend had seen no one from the bishopric or Relief Society nor even received a phone call. He had no contact with anyone outside the family, not even from his closest friends. It was as if his son didn't exist and was already dead and buried. I have had similar feelings at various times in my own life, but I understand the awkward feelings of others in trying to deal with individuals who have mental illness.

The realization of being alone as you deal with someone suffering a bout of suicidal depression is heartbreaking. Casseroles are taken to those suffering from cancer, surgery, or new mothers. These life events appear to be the qualifying measure of suffering or celebration, whereas having a brain disorder such as depression does not. Mental illness is socially unacceptable.

Several things helped us. First there was the blessing of education about mental illness that we received from the National Alliance for the Mentally Ill. Next, our ward family and true friends eventually took part in the rallying cry of activity within our own home. We heard the sounds of true sisterhood united in voices together in cleaning bathrooms, the smell of baking in the kitchen, and a washing machine and vacuum running. The phone would ring and voices would gently inquire and briefly encourage us. These were voices of angels.

Ought we not to become experts in this process? Our religious culture is best when facing adversity that threatens our survival as a whole, but how are we when suffering individually? How do we react when someone is quietly suffering with a mental illness? I've learned that others can help a person with mental illness most effectively by showing patience and love.

The Five "Be's" of Helping

First and foremost, *be a friend.* Many people are frightened by mental illness. Befriend those who have a mental illness and those that love them.

Second, *refuse to support the discrimination* and stigma that so often are associated with mental illness. Don't make fun of or belittle those with emotional problems.

Third, *be a part of the solution and support system.* Help those with mental illness and their families connect with the resources they need— for example, LDS Family Services, which can be accessed through their bishop. Encourage family members to support the healing process and professional counseling. Professional help is fundamental to recovery. Many community-based programs at local mental health centers set the proper environments for treatment and are less restrictive than a general hospital.

Fourth, *be compassionate and supportive without judgment.* Excellent parents of mentally ill children are often told by the unknowing that perhaps the child's illness could have been avoided had they been "better" parents. Recent scientific evidence clearly shows that biological components in mental health disorders is far beyond intervention by wise parenting alone. There are proven physical, chemical, and electrical differences in the brains of those afflicted with mental illness.

Fifth and finally, *be informed.* Learn about brain disorders and resources. Laws such as the Family Medical Leave Act and the Americans with Disabilities Act, as well as numerous special school programs, may assist individuals suffering with mental illness. Such "hidden" resources will facilitate the healing process of all involved.

We found the best individuals to learn from were those who had the same belief and faith system we did. We were absolutely stunned to learn how many around us were in similar circumstances. They had built the same barriers we had built, and for the same reasons. We, like they, had built the walls as the impact of mental illness overtook our lives. Parents who had previously been through the same kind of experience came as gifts, bringing insights and answers we had prayed for.

It is well known that a combination of counseling and medical attention has the best benefit. It may be short term or long term, but it has been our experience that treatment for mental illness is often a process of elimination, even with the best credentialed specialists. The use of medication often involved a change in sleeping habits and diets. We learned to be flexible and patient just as we would if we had to learn about the treatment of some other disease, such as diabetes, heart disease, or multiple sclerosis. Mental illness is a disease like any other that could have affected our son.

My Mom and Dad

One of the main lessons my wife and I have been taught throughout this challenge has been that we are in this as an entire family. My own mother and father have been my saving grace. They have been a constant example of calm and purity of heart. In every context they lived in a way that has taught me as a parent. They had taught me, "Never lock your heart, and never lock your door." Nevertheless, proper limits were needed, and they were set within our home. Tough love has its place, and it has been exercised at times by us in proper measure.

My father has often quoted the lifting words of a Quaker proverb: "Thee lift me and I'll lift thee, and we will ascend together" (Robert D. Hales, "'Return with Honor,'" *Ensign,* July 1994, 48). In some miraculous way my son, because of his mental illness, has lifted me. I believe that someday we as a family can ascend together. I pray each of us will gain the strength to keep this goal foremost in our lives. I believe that with the loving support of my wife, children, parents, and friends I will meet faithfully the challenges that remain ahead. I truly believe that parents, spouses and families can cope with mental illness by learning patience, unconditional love, and true compassion. I believe we are given such challenges for the blessing of all involved. We do need each other. That was one of the main lessons we all had to learn individually: we were all in this together as an entire family unit.

Testimony

Pretending the problem of mental illness doesn't exist or will right itself without outside help is like crushing a tender dried rose preserved after a special occasion. The rose was meant to be carefully brought out, a memento of a treasured experience to be shared with others. I have learned that if you're not careful, it will be flung about and splintered because it was misunderstood or unappreciated by another.

My wife and I have been taught daily as we have learned and adjusted to the myriad issues that come into play when living with mental illness. The Lord has promised that our weaknesses can become strengths and that "all things shall work together for [our] good" if we search and pray (Ether 12:27; D&C 90:24). There is comfort in the knowledge that we are able to turn to the Lord. There is an immense upwelling of support that amazingly comes as needed after we have individually done all that we can, confessed our love, and demonstrated our faith to the Lord.

Please don't try to carry this burden alone. You cannot do it alone, and I cannot do it alone; but together we can lift each other, and we will ascend together.

Dedicated to my sons, Michael, Mathew, and Andrew; my daughters, Emilie and Mary; my sweet wife of twenty-six years, Susan; and my parents, Elder Robert Dean and Mary Crandall Hales, who are living examples of love and forgiveness.

ANXIETY AND RELATED DISORDERS

Common types of anxiety disorders include generalized anxiety disorder, obsessive compulsive disorder (OCD), post-traumatic stress disorder (PTSD), panic disorder, social anxiety disorder (social phobia), and specific phobias. Anxiety disorders are the most common psychiatric illnesses affecting both children and adults. Anxiety disorders cause people to feel frightened, distressed, and uneasy for no apparent reason.

Symptoms

Generalized Anxiety Disorder

- Chronic, exaggerated worry about everyday, routine life events and activities, lasting at least six months.

- Almost always anticipating the worst even though there is little reason to expect it.

- Accompanied by physical symptoms, such as fatigue, trembling, muscle tension, headache, or nausea.

Obsessive-Compulsive Disorder

- Repeated, intrusive, and unwanted thoughts or rituals that seem impossible to control.

Panic Disorder

- Characterized by panic attacks, sudden feelings of terror that strike repeatedly and without warning.

- Physical symptoms include chest pain, heart palpitations, shortness of breath, dizziness, abdominal discomfort, feelings of unreality, and fear of dying.

Post-traumatic Stress Disorder

- Persistent symptoms that occur after experiencing such traumatic events as war, rape, child abuse, natural disasters, or being taken hostage.

- Nightmares, flashbacks, numbing of emotions, and depression; feeling angry, irritable, and distracted; and being easily startled.

Social Anxiety Disorder (Social Phobia)

- Extreme disabling and irrational fear of something that really poses little or no actual danger; the fear leads to avoidance of objects or situations and can cause sufferers to limit their lives.

Specific Phobia Disorder

- Intense fear reaction to a specific object or situation such as dogs, spiders, or heights.

- The level of fear is usually inappropriate to the situation, and is recognized by the sufferer as being irrational.

Life Is Just What You Make It

Donny Osmond

Donny Osmond has worked in the entertainment industry for decades as a singer, songwriter, musician, actor, and television show host. He and his wife, Debbie, have five sons. In this chapter, he shares his story about panic attacks.

By early 1995, I had been with *Joseph and the Technicolor Dream Coat* more than two and a half years. Although playing the role was essentially doing the same thing every show, no performance was ever exactly like any other. Unlike singing in concert, where there is always room for improvisation and small errors, acting, singing, and dancing with a large cast is an exercise in precision and timing. Not to say we each didn't slip up occasionally; we did. And with live performances, there's a healthy amount of nervousness all performers experience.

Sometime around 1994, I began feeling a kind of anxiousness that was unlike anything I'd ever felt before. I'd been a little nervous about every one of my performances all my life, but there were ways I could circumvent the anxiety. For as long as I can remember—whether I was onstage or in a business meeting—I knew that if I just got that applause at the end of the first song, a laugh when I made a joke, my nervousness would diminish, though never go away. I'd been through the wringer so many times, before and after "Soldier of Love," that I didn't feel like the same person anymore. It was a feeling I couldn't quite pinpoint or articulate. No matter where I was, I felt subordinate to other people and uncertain, especially in business situations.

The only time I ever felt really confident was in the recording studio. Each time I put on the headphones, I'd go into another world, a state of flow, so to speak. As I'd listen to the playback I knew I could sing. That wasn't the problem. But sometimes I felt that was the only thing about my career that I really did know. Everything else was a mystery, and by the time *Joseph* came to me, I was more emotionally battered and scarred than I realized. Ironically, it was during *Joseph*—when, professionally, things looked like they couldn't have possibly gone better—that the nervousness began taking a new form. Opening night in Chicago during "Any Dream Will Do"—the second number in the show and the first in which I appear—I stopped singing, hoping the children's chorus would be loud enough to carry the note I couldn't sing. I didn't know what was happening to me, but I couldn't control my voice. So I stopped singing altogether and just mouthed the words.

By far the worst episode occurred while I was onstage in Chicago in 1994. One of the show-stopping numbers was "Song of the King," which featured Johnny Seaton portraying the King of Egypt as the King of Rock and Roll. Pharaoh begged Joseph to interpret his troubled dreams. I was kneeling before Johnny with my back to the audience, getting ready to sing "Pharaoh's Dream Explained," when the room started spinning around me and I was sure I would black out. The night before, I had blown the lyrics to the song that was coming up, and the fear that it might happen again loomed larger and larger as the music played and my cue got closer.

Unless you've experienced a panic attack yourself, you might find it hard to understand what it feels like, but bear with me as I try to explain. Once the fear of embarrassing myself grabbed me, I couldn't get loose. It was as if a bizarre and terrifying unreality had replaced everything that was familiar and safe. I felt powerless to think or reason my way out of the panic. It had a whole strange, hallucinatory quality to it. For example, I could see myself down on the stage as if I were flying above it all, but I couldn't get back "inside" myself and take control. In the grip of my wildest fears, I was paralyzed, certain that if I made one wrong move, I would literally die. Even more terrifying, I'd have felt relieved to die.

Kneeling before Johnny, I kept trying to remember the words, but they slipped through my fingers like mercury, defying me to try again. The harder I tried, the more elusive they became. The best I could do was to not black out, and I got through the show, barely, by telling myself repeatedly, *Stay conscious, stay conscious.* Another time, the only way I got through the ballad "Close Every Door" was by envisioning my late Grandma Davis's face and imagining having a conversation with her as I went through the motions of the song. And these attacks of nerves weren't just about performing onstage. I remember being so wound up at the prospect of co-hosting *Live! with Regis & Kathie Lee* that I didn't sleep at all the night before and got nauseous right before I went on. Later, when

I learned to "rank" my panic attacks on a scale of 1 to 10, these would all qualify as 10s. Another time, my anxiety was so overwhelming that during my audition to play the voice of Hercules in the Disney animated feature, my performance was embarrassing. It was one of those moments when I started to wonder if I could continue a singing career at all.

Something was definitely wrong, and at first I clung to a "reasonable explanation": the schedule, the commuting back and forth, the fact that I was living so much of my life away from Debbie and the boys, my responsibility to a successful show. But deep inside, I knew that none of it made sense. I'd performed under every adverse condition imaginable. I'd carried a good deal of responsibility since I was a child. Why couldn't I do it now? I wasn't on tour. I knew the show backwards and forwards. The audience was back, and they accepted me just fine. So why was everything suddenly going so terribly wrong?

By the time we reached Minneapolis in early 1995, I was pretty certain that the stress of being away from my family and the weekly round-trip flights were wearing me down. Either that, or I was just losing my mind. Everything was beginning to annoy me. I would be short-tempered with people and sometimes even suspicious of them, which is not my style. What did they want from me? Why couldn't they leave me alone?

I was in my dressing room, sitting at my makeup table when I heard our stage manager Dianne Woodrow announce, "Fifteen minutes to curtain." By then my routine was down pat—the makeup, the wig, the costume. Every night it went off without a hitch. This night, though, I sat at my makeup table paralyzed. I just couldn't bring myself to do anything. I felt sick and clammy with sweat. I looked down at my hands; they were shaking. When Giovanna, the woman who did my hair, came in to put on my wig, the glue wouldn't even stick to my forehead, I was sweating so much.

"Are you sick?" she asked.

I couldn't answer.

When I heard "Five minutes to curtain," the panic rose until I didn't know what I was doing. In a fit of rage, I picked up every jar, bottle, can, brush, mirror—whatever I found on my dressing table—and threw it all at the wall, screaming. I caught my reflection in the mirror and thought, *Who is that man?* Then I dropped back into my seat, put my head down on the table, and started bawling. My friend and dresser,

Stephen McMulkin, found Dianne and told her, "Something's wrong with Donny."

Dianne rushed in, took one look at the room, and knew something was terribly wrong. "What do you want to do, Donny?" My mind raced back and forth: *Yes, I can do this. No, I can't. I can pull myself together. No, I'm falling apart. I can go on. No, I can't.* I just couldn't get a grip, and even as I said, "No, I'll be okay. I'm going on," I knew I wouldn't. I was relieved to hear Dianne say, "No, you're not going on." It was like someone was giving me permission not to have to live through the panic.

They announced that I would be unable to perform that night, and just five minutes after the regular curtain time, my understudy, Vance Avery, went on. The funny thing about it was, once I knew I didn't have to go onstage, the panic evaporated. I felt fine, like I could do anything in the world—except, of course, walk on the stage.

The anxiety waxed and waned. Some nights I went on and everything was fine. I confided in Debbie, of course, over the phone, and in Jill Willis, who was there in Minneapolis. They could see that I needed help, but what kind of help? I couldn't even articulate what I was feeling. I was nervous, but after thirty years of going onstage, how could that be possible? And, besides this was something way beyond anything you could call stage fright. There was more to it than that. I couldn't stop agonizing over the craziest things. I'd lie in bed at night wondering. *What if . . . ?* And then imagine a series of possible events that might unfold, all of them culminating in my being humiliated. I kept myself awake for hours, mentally plotting elaborate, labyrinthine strategies, plans, and contingencies so that no matter what happened, I would be in control.

What made it even more maddening is that there wasn't a shred of logic behind my thinking. No one was asking me to defend myself now. I was exactly where I always wanted to be. And there were moments when, intellectually, I knew that. Emotionally, though, it was a completely different story. Once my mind took off on something, it was as if I'd been kidnapped and tied to a roller coaster. I couldn't stop it. Naturally, the sleep deprivation only made everything else worse. I had to do something.

One morning, I phoned Jill at six o'clock, crying so hard I could barely speak. "I don't know what's wrong with me," I whispered, "but I have to go home. I have to go home." After a few days' rest, home in

Utah, I felt ready to go back to work, but something still was not right. I tried acupuncture, which helped a little. I even managed to fall into a dead sleep during treatments, but I was feeling more jittery. It was a vicious cycle, because as my emotions and my behavior became more threatening to me, I tried even harder to suppress them. Next we tried homeopathy, and Jill found a reputable practitioner who prescribed an herbal concoction diluted in a few teaspoons of vodka. I don't know how much it helped, but it was weird to think that I was drinking "legally." Like the acupuncture, we reasoned that this was noninvasive and safe. The worst that could happen was it wouldn't work and I'd be back where I started. But that didn't help much either.

My state of mind was deteriorating so rapidly, I seriously started to consider drinking alcohol for real. I was that desperate. I know for most people this would be no big deal, but, in light of my beliefs, for me it was. I didn't even know what it felt like to drink, but in my worst moments, I'd recall people saying how it relaxed them and made them forget their problems. That was all I needed to hear.

Then I lost it.

My "weekends" home had been expanded to include Mondays and Tuesdays. I usually left Utah early Wednesday morning to fly back to Minneapolis for that night's show. Of course, I never looked forward to saying good-bye to my family, but suddenly I was beginning to dread it. At first, a general uneasiness would settle over me like a fog, beginning a few hours before my flight. Then it would begin the night before, then it would keep me awake nights until most of the time at home I was completely focused on—obsessed with—leaving and being so afraid to go.

One Tuesday night, I was lying in bed awake, shivering, in a cold sweat. I scared Debbie to death, because neither of us knew what was going on. Debbie's father, with whom I'm very close, came over and talked to me to see if he could help. I calmed down a little, but Debbie insisted we go to the emergency room anyway. Something was seriously wrong. I was deathly afraid of something, but I didn't know what. And the more I tried to tell myself there was nothing to be afraid of, the more afraid I became.

By the time we got to the hospital, I was damp with sweat and shaking uncontrollably, so hard that I almost couldn't walk. Some unnamed, unknown fear had my heart racing. The closer it got to daybreak and my flight back to Minneapolis, the more violent the shaking became and the colder I felt. I was taken to a private examination room, where they hooked me up to an EKG to be sure I wasn't having a heart attack and drew blood for tests. Lying on the table, I remember waiting for the doctor to give me the results. Secretly, I was hoping he would tell me that I had a disease that meant I could never go onstage again. I was ready to hear anything.

"Mr. Osmond, I have some good news," the doctor said a couple of hours later. "There's nothing wrong with you." Instead of breathing a sigh of relief, I was thrown into another panic, because if there was nothing physically wrong with me, then my worst fear had been confirmed: I was going crazy.

"All you need to do is take a break"—which was impossible, because of my schedule—"maybe you need to go on a long vacation and go fishing." I hate fishing. The doctor gave me some pills, some kind of sedative, and sent me on my way.

I got dressed, and as I walked out of the hospital, Debbie remembers that I was smiling and cracking jokes to make every one laugh. "It was like Donny still had to be onstage," she recalled. I'd always found it easier to relax if I did something to make people like me, and this was no different. Slowly it began to dawn on me that I'd been doing this my whole life. What was I doing? What was I so afraid of?

We got home, both shaken and scared. "I've got to get to Minneapolis and do the show," I told Debbie.

"You can't do the show," she said. "You are not doing the show."

"I have to, Debbie. I have to go. You know what kind of complaints I'm going to get from people if I'm not on that stage. What will people think of me if I miss a show? And you know the kind of pressure I get from the producer when I'm not there."

"Well, if you're going, I'm going with you."

A few hours later, Debbie and I were en route to Minneapolis, not that I had any idea where we were. The pills had taken effect, and I was so out of it, Debbie practically had to carry me through the Denver airport, where we caught a connecting flight. I slept the entire trip. Once we got to my apartment and the medication wore off enough, I started making plans to go on that night. "I've got to do it," I told Debbie.

She disagreed with me, but I insisted and I did go on that night. It was one of the most difficult challenges I have ever faced. But for the next three days, I sat with Debbie and cried, asking her probably a hundred times, "How am I going to get through this?" and begging her not to tell anyone. I would have done anything to make the pain go away.

"Donny, why do you feel that you have to be perfect onstage?" Debbie asked.

I looked at her. It seemed like such a crazy question. I had to be perfect because I had to be perfect. Wasn't it obvious? It was expected of me.

"Donny, you don't have to be perfect. The people in the audience don't know how you think the performance is supposed to be. If you mess up a line or make a little mistake, who knows? Who cares? And do you really believe that people will think less of you because you're not perfect?"

I thought, and I hate to admit it, but the answer was, Yes, I did think people would stop liking me if I wasn't trying to be perfect. It was ridiculous and irrational, of course, but it was real to me. Debbie had watched this whole process evolve over the years, and she knew me so well that years after that night in the emergency room, she could say that she wasn't surprised at what happened to me. I would later discover that most people who knew me well weren't surprised, either. That's when Debbie said the words I needed to hear: "Just go out there and be average." I would never want to be just average, but at least now I had permission not to be perfect.

Though I hadn't missed that many performances, everyone at Live Entertainment, the company that produced *Joseph,* was concerned. As fate would have it, there had been an actor in another of the company's productions, *The Phantom of the Opera,* who had suffered symptoms similar to mine. Dan Brambilla, an executive who worked for Live Entertainment, had the name and phone number of a psychotherapist, Dr. Jerilyn Ross, who specialized in treating what most of us would call stage fright. For the past several months, I'd tried everything I could to avoid seeing a psychologist. I needed help, but in the back of my mind I worried that my problem would end up in the press and everything I'd worked so hard to build back up would crumble to dust.

After I learned that there were many other performers Dr. Ross had treated, I relaxed a little. Besides, I'd reached a dead end. If I didn't stop this madness, it was all going to be over for me, anyway.

We had just closed in Minneapolis and moved on to Toronto, for our third run there. Dr. Ross flew to Toronto before opening night to work with me. The most amazing thing about meeting her was that I finally found someone who understood exactly what I was going through. No fear or belief I told her about struck her as unusual or bizarre. Not only had she been treating people like me for years, but she herself had once suffered from severe anxiety attacks. When I discovered that I was not the only person in the world like this, it was like someone had given me a second chance at life. There was a name for what was happening to me—social phobia—and a course of treatment. I can't even imagine what my life would have been like had I not found Dr. Ross.

She explained to me that social phobia is one of several common anxiety disorders. People who suffer from social phobia are afraid to do anything in public—including walking down a street, eating in a restaurant, or asking someone for directions—because they fear they will be ridiculed. It's not unusual for someone with a social phobia to believe that people are watching them wherever they go, whatever they do, and that they are laughing at them as well. For most people, this is an irrational fear. No one is looking at them or laughing at them. In my case, however, there was an element of reality to my otherwise irrational fears that had to be considered as well. From an early age, I was being looked at wherever I went. And I was laughed at as well. But, as Dr. Ross demonstrated to me, my mind took things that were real and exaggerated and distorted them. In the grip of panic, I experienced an internally generated fantasy, not reality.

Treatment for social phobia involves learning to identify the conditions that result in an attack and then discovering the techniques you use to bring that anxiety to a manageable level. Therapists who treat this use talk therapy in conjunction with cognitive behavioral therapy. The goal of this treatment is not so much tracing how the phobia began or why you suffer from it, but teaching you practical ways of dealing with it. Sometimes this involves facing your fear under controlled circumstances, or teaching yourself to stop your irrational thoughts before they take hold. Social phobia is not a condition that can be "cured" the same way you cure a disease. It's always there. Just by teaching me that I wasn't alone and that there was a way out for me, Dr. Ross changed—

maybe even saved—my life.

Over the next couple of weeks, the panic came on a few times, but I found that the more I practiced managing it, the easier it became. More important, though, I stopped becoming anxious before the fact.

Between getting a grip on my social phobia and going into my fifth year with *Joseph,* I was finally letting myself enjoy the success.

Finally, and above all, I want to thank my Heavenly Father and His son, Jesus Christ, for blessing me beyond measure.

From Donny Osmond, *Donny Osmond: Life Is Just What You Make It—My Story So Far* (New York: Hyperion, 1999); used by permission.

Close to Home

Name Withheld

The author is a retired mental health therapist. He is married and the father of five children. He tells of his wife's experience with an anxiety disorder.

During Memorial Day weekend in 1994, my family and I were on a camping trip. We were having a relaxed and wonderful time. It was 2:30 Sunday morning and everyone was asleep—at least I thought so. Suddenly I awoke to hear strange sounds coming from my wife. She was sitting up in bed next to me gasping for air, clutching her throat. "I can't breathe," she told me between gasps. "My throat is closed off!" She was starting to panic and cry. Then I started to panic. Nothing like this had ever happened in our nearly thirty years of marriage.

Our two youngest children woke up alarmed, asking what was wrong with Mother. The youngest child began to cry. Our teenage daughter was still half asleep and bewildered with this strange happening in the middle of the night.

Fortunately, my training as a mental health professional with some years of experience and a little emergency medical training helped me to get control of myself and then to calmly take control of the situation. In what seemed like an eternity but in reality was only a matter of minutes, I was able to calm my children and discover that there were no obstructions in my wife's throat. I loosened clothing that inhibited her breathing, turned on a fan, and opened a window to give her plenty of fresh air. Finally I convinced her to lie back on some pillows and breathe slowly. She was sweating and trembling. She was able to tell me that she had chest pains, felt dizzy and light-headed, and had experienced chills just before her throat closed off. Now she was experiencing hot flashes. I suspected a panic attack, something that I had dealt with over the years with my clients. A panic attack didn't fit with what I knew about her—or thought I knew.

I asked myself, "Why such an unexpected attack in the middle of the night?" There should have been signs the day before. I helped her get dressed for a possible trip to the closest hospital. She assured me there was nothing she could recall that might have triggered the attack. She was as surprised as anyone, but she kept complaining of chest pains and having difficulty breathing. Those were signs of possible heart problems. I wasn't taking any chances. We transported her to the small local hospital.

After a thorough examination of my wife, the doctor ruled out a heart attack and said that he could find nothing wrong. He suspected gas in the stomach and prescribed antacid medication for her. Not satisfied with his diagnosis, I asked a lot of questions. The doctor wouldn't even consider a possible panic attack or other related issues. He assured us, however, that nothing was wrong with her heart and lungs. She was breathing much better now, so we left the hospital. The antacid medication did nothing more than soothe her throat. A slow, long walk around the neighborhood of the small rural town in the early morning hours and laughing about the experience turned out to be helpful, although some of the residents probably didn't appreciate our early morning antics.

I had worked at a mental health agency for many years as a counselor. During my career I received a lot of training from the agency and other professional organizations. I also maintained a part-time private caseload of clients (now a full-time practice). During those years, I counseled people with all kinds of social and emotional issues. I felt competent in my skills in helping people with mental health concerns. Still, even with all my training and experience, I was caught off guard when I first saw my wife have that panic attack. I had never anticipated such problems striking so close to home to someone so near and dear to me.

I was aware that my wife had a history of allergies and asthma was in her family background. I was also aware that she couldn't stand being in enclosed places. She had an intense fear of heights and flying and was fearful of being alone. She taught classes at church and gave talks, but these were difficult things for her to do because of her fears. But the panic attacks made me realize something more serious was happening with my wife.

Before breaking camp at the lake and heading back to our home, my wife experienced two other "attacks." Neither of the attacks was as serious as the first one. We did determine that there was nothing in the fresh spring air at the campground that had caused her problems. In fact, if anything it helped. Stomach gas, or "heartburn," as the doctor had diagnosed, didn't fit the symptoms either.

Once back home, a thorough examination by her doctor disclosed that my wife was in excellent physical condition but that she had indeed experienced a series of panic attacks, an anxiety disorder of no small proportion. A referral was made to a local psychiatrist, who confirmed the diagnosis and prescribed a medication. He also suggested therapy to deal with her anxiety. At first I had mixed feelings as a mental health professional with my wife having to see a psychiatrist and being referred to a therapist because of her panic. Of course, being her husband and living close to the situation, I knew it was not ethical and certainly not wise for me to be her therapist, even though I knew what treatment might be helpful for her.

Much to my chagrin, I learned that I didn't know as much about my dear wife nor her background as I thought I did. Even after five children and years of marriage, I discovered I really didn't know that much about her emotional history, her fears, or her innermost feelings.

For years my wife had been fighting "silent battles" with anxiety and panic. She had chosen not to disclose them to me or anyone else because of embarrassment and for fear of what it might do to our relationship. She didn't want to be misjudged or thought less of by our children or by our extended families or by her friends. After all, she was (and still is) a skilled musician and a perfectionist. Why would she want to risk showing or telling anyone that she had anxiety and depression and experienced panic attacks? She had suffered so much for so long, and I didn't even know it! How had I missed all of this? That experience at the lake campground opened the floodgate to her silent suffering. Thank goodness!

I had learned over the years as a therapist that I couldn't "treat" my wife for emotional problems in the same manner that I did my clients. Once I became aware of my wife's condition I made every effort to be a caring and supportive husband. I tried not to overreact or counsel her in what she should do. That was a hard thing to do with someone as close to you as your wife, especially when you think you know the answers to her problems.

I felt that my hands were tied. I learned that when I reacted to her panic and anxiety, it simply added more stress to the situation and made it worse. I learned quickly that my concern about her condition only added more fuel to an already burning fire. Hence, I became a better listener, became more attentive and calm with her, and rather than trying to "fix" things, I proceeded cautiously, allowing my wife to discover the best solutions to her problems.

The famous saying by Galileo, which has always been a standard to me in my counseling practice, struck home to me in a personal way: "You cannot teach a person anything. You can only help them find it within themselves." Only when she inquired did I introduce her to materials and books about panic attacks, anxiety disorders, and even depression, which I thought might help her find answers. When she first started reading about the symptoms and causes of her emotional problems, however, she became frustrated because reading about them only brought on the symptoms in her again. I had to let her do it in her own time and way.

Exercising patience and being nonjudgmental were not easy for me. My wife and I have been married for more than thirty-five years. In the earlier years of our marriage there were times I was impatient and critical. As a new husband I recall struggling when she exhibited some of those hard-to-understand behaviors or phobias that accompany anxiety. For example, my first inclination when those behaviors occurred would be to say or think something such as, "That's foolishness! What do you mean we have to leave the bedroom door open?" or "That doesn't make sense! Why can't we fly instead of drive to California?" And the list of my critical statements went on and on. Learning to live with my wife's anxiety and panic taught me to be patient and understanding. I've never personally experienced severe anxiety or panic. But when it came that close to home I could understand in a small way the intense fear it generated.

After the camping experience I became aware of a number of my wife's panic attacks. Eventually I became quite skilled at helping her through them, but only after she had asked for help. I learned to keep her calm and have her breathe slowly. I encouraged her to take deep breaths. I would talk slowly and quietly. Instead of having her sit or lie down and relax as one might expect, I discovered that she actually coped better by *doing* something, such as walking or putting together a puzzle. We are all different. I also learned that just to be close to her and to hold her was helpful.

I knew from my experience that after ten or fifteen minutes the panic would pass and things would return to normal. I'm convinced the most difficult challenge for me personally was "listening" to her rather than "counseling" her. It took some time, but I became more patient and a better listener. There is an old saying that goes: "The Lord blessed us with two ears and one mouth. We should learn to listen twice as much as we talk!" It took patience, but I slowly came to heed that wise bit of counsel.

These types of emotional concerns can destroy a family. Our children didn't understand their mom's symptoms at first. Many times my wife and I talked to our five children about her panic attacks and anxiety. I tried to educate them about these issues and to help them understand and to be patient with their mom. We prayed for help from Heavenly Father that they might understand and be supportive. It worked.

Over the years, we developed a system of support that seemed to help. Carefully selected family members and close friends became a great resource to her. I knew I couldn't always be with her. When she would have one of her "bad days" and I wasn't available to talk or come home, she would often turn to these resources for support. They were wonderful, caring, and most helpful. My wife will always be grateful to them—and so will I!

I learned that to help my wife I had to be healthy myself. When things got rough, I would take "a time-out." I made sure I took time for myself. I had (and still have) several hobbies, such as golfing, fishing, and skiing. I tried to stay on a regular exercise regimen or do something physically strenuous. I tell my clients (and believe personally) that you have to learn to play as hard as you work. Enduring and coping with life's challenges is hard work. I've always been a strong advocate of giving yourself "space" and time to regenerate yourself. Sometimes as part of my time-out, I go to my "personal grove." My grove is a small group of trees in a nearby mountain pass. I go there to think, pray, and be alone.

Humor has also been a great time-out activity for me. On more difficult days, I might come home and watch a funny show, or sometimes I would find a joke or something else that would cause me to laugh. When I didn't take time-outs, I would get down quickly. I know I am a better help to my wife when I make time for myself.

One of our most dramatic experiences was when our youngest daughter left to serve a mission. My wife was supportive of her leaving, but she was very close to this daughter, as she was the last one to leave home. My wife struggled to have her gone. She cried a lot and would wake up in the middle of the night feeling panicky and fearful. She would walk the floors of our home for many hours or put puzzles together to try to overcome her feelings of anxiety. I was anxious, too—anxious that my wife was anxious. After having a difficulty coping with this situation, I contacted our family doctor, who put my wife on medication again. That helped considerably. I also remember giving her countless priesthood blessings, assisted by a home teacher, a neighbor, an extended family member, or another ward member. These helped immensely. Both my wife and I have great faith in the power of the priesthood and our Heavenly Father. Because of these wonderful resources, she improved.

A couple of scriptures helped me to cope. The first one is found in Doctrine and Covenants 4:6: "Remember faith, virtue, knowledge, temperance, patience, brotherly kindness, godliness, charity, humility, diligence." I memorized the words on my mission, but I learned what they really meant as I helped myself and my wife through these difficult experiences. The second scripture is Doctrine and Covenants 121:42–43: "By kindness, and pure knowledge, which shall greatly enlarge the soul without hypocrisy, and without guile—Reproving betimes with sharpness when moved upon by the Holy Ghost." Many times when I would become upset and want to criticize my wife for her anxiety and panic-related behaviors, I would ask myself, *Are you being moved upon by the Holy Ghost?* Of course, the answer was usually *no.* I would realize I was being moved upon by anger, frustration, and discouragement. Once I realized that, I was able to stop the criticism. I became a kinder and gentler husband. I have repeated these scriptures many times in my mind and heart over the years.

My wife and I have learned much about panic attacks and other anxiety disorders. We have read books and asked many questions. We have learned that a significant number of medical doctors and a surprising number of mental health professionals don't know as much about these disorders as we thought they would. We've discovered that at least some anxiety disorders are often misdiagnosed and mistreated by presumably well-trained and competent professionals.

We've also learned that willpower alone isn't enough to cure panic and anxiety. They ofttimes require medications, therapy, and a host of self-help methods. For sure, priesthood blessings, prayers, and supportive family members and friends are required. But even with all of these helps, my wife still at times experiences symptoms of anxiety and panic. It's just that now she has learned how to manage them much better. And I have learned to cope better. . . . I think!

I've had a church calling all of my adult life. I've been a bishop, a counselor to a mission president, and a high councilor, among other callings, and I've been able to function quite well in all of these despite my wife's challenges. She has always been supportive of me in these callings and has never wanted to be a burden, nor has she. During her hard times, I found it important to stay close to her, to have long talks and to go on long walks or rides together. She knew I would always be there for her. She certainly has been for me!

I frequently ponder on the temple covenants and promises I made years ago. I remember promising to be with her "through sickness." I've come to know this means any type of sickness, physical or mental. I have a great hope of an eternal marriage. I love my wife very much. I want to be with her throughout eternity. I have hope in the plan of salvation that her panic and anxiety will one day be overcome.

One might falsely believe that my wife's panic and anxiety are a sacrifice or a burden. They are not. More and more I see them as wonderful blessings. Because of the challenges we have faced, we have learned to depend on our Heavenly Father. It has bonded us as a couple in a special way. It has helped me understand the sacred parts of our souls and of our marriage covenants. I have the assurance that we will be in eternity together if we can endure our challenges today, one day at a time.

I give most of the credit by far to my dear wife. She has had a great attitude, a strong will, and an unbelievable determination through all of this. She has learned to manage her panic attacks and anxiety quite well. She has tremendous faith that Heavenly Father answers prayers. She knows that there is hope in healing through the atonement of Jesus Christ, as do I. There is hope. There is always hope.

SCHIZOPHRENIA AND RELATED DISORDERS

There are several types of schizophrenia and related psychotic disorders. The more common disorders include paranoid schizophrenia, disorganized schizophrenia, delusional disorder, schizoaffective disorder, and postpartum psychosis. Schizophrenia and related psychotic disorders are brain disorders that interfere with a person's ability to think clearly, manage emotions, make decisions, and relate to others.

Symptoms of Schizophrenia

Schizophrenia symptoms are classified into two groups: *positive* symptoms and *negative* symptoms.

Positive symptoms are disturbances that are *added* to an individual's personality:

- Delusions—false ideas. Individuals may believe that someone is spying on them or that they are someone famous.

- Hallucinations—seeing, feeling, tasting, hearing or smelling something that doesn't really exist. The most common experience is hearing imaginary voices that give commands or comments to the individual.

- Disordered thinking and speech—moving from one topic to another in a nonsensical fashion. Individuals may make up their own words or sounds.

Negative symptoms are capabilities that are *lost* from the person's personality:

- Social withdrawal.

- Extreme apathy.

- Lack of drive or initiative.

- Emotional unresponsiveness.

- Loss of contact with reality.

Modern-day Lepers

Name Withheld

The author, who is a widow with children, serves in her ward as a nursery leader. She tells her own story of coping with schizophrenia.

I thought my life would be a Mormon fairy tale that would end "happily ever after." I was married on August 21, 1970, in the Salt Lake Temple. My husband was a tall, handsome, returned missionary. I thought my husband and I had the greatest future together. I thought life would be easy and that all our children would turn out really well and the Church would be the center of our lives. I believed our family home evenings and scripture study would be wonderful. I have always believed in fasting and prayer. I had fasted and prayed to our Heavenly Father to make sure I would make the correct choice in this all-important matter of marriage. Furthermore, my husband had fasted and prayed about his choice of a marriage partner, and it was manifested to him that I was the correct choice. We both felt that we had made the right choice.

After we were married, we both continued our education at Brigham Young University. I graduated with a bachelor's degree in elementary education and then had a darling baby girl in December 1971. We had a cute red-headed baby boy on October 4, 1973. I had always wanted a large family. I had thirteen pregnancies in sixteen years, but only six of the pregnancies resulted in live births.

I wanted to be a stay-at-home mother and be there for my children when they needed my help and advice. I thought after they had grown, I might endeavor to teach part time, but my main goal was to be a full-time mother and live this fairy tale.

Problems in our marriage surfaced during my thirteenth pregnancy because of gestational diabetes. I had to have insulin shots and monitor my blood glucose level every couple of hours. It was a precarious situation that threatened the life of the baby, but the baby arrived okay.

In the spring of 1988, I had a feeling that something was seriously wrong with my husband. I felt that he had some sexual addictions. I lived in great fear that he would molest my children. I wasn't sleeping at night, and I felt overwhelmed. I went to several therapists, but they didn't help my situation very much. I still felt constant fear.

Then I started to do something that proved detrimental to my mental health. I didn't realize it at the time, but later I recognized my great error in the matter. I read two books that were recommended to me. I read them hoping that I might find some solutions to my problems. One was *Betrayal of Innocence,* which went into the heinous sexual assault that adults force on innocent children. The second book was *People of the Lie,* by Scott Peck. I started to believe in the concepts of these books—that most people are hypocrites and liars. In my mind I imagined that most of the people in my area were like the wicked people of King Noah in the Book of Mormon.

Things got worse. I kicked my husband out of our home. I thought he was Satan. I wasn't sleeping at all. I thought the Lord would provide me with a new husband. I thought my husband was going to be my bishop. I was reading the Book of Mormon night and day. I was listening to spiritual music, grasping at any straw for help. I thought this was the end of the world and God was going to consume the world and burn up all the people. I thought it was time for him to come and get me. These thoughts were real to me. I felt that except for a few people, most were wicked and evil and molesting their children.

On June 29, 1988, I totally lost touch with reality. I took my four youngest children—aged nine, five, two, and two-and-a-half-months—up a mountain. My thoughts were racing like a speeding car. I was proclaiming profanities at all the people I met. I believed that it was the second coming of the Savior, and he would cleanse the world from sin.

We parked our car and started walking up the mountain. I didn't know where I was. I thought my husband had put a bomb in my car and it was going to explode. My children believed me. I remember on that mountain feeling so glad the Lord was saving us. On the mountain I made an altar of rocks and placed the baby on it. I made the kids sit down and pray. As I look back on those actions now, I realize I was in a different world. But no one could have told me these things weren't true.

I stripped my clothes off and took off my children's clothes because I thought we wouldn't need them when the Savior came for us. I was still screaming profanities on the mountaintop when a policeman climbed up to help us. I threw rocks at the police officer. He finally helped calm me down, and he called an ambulance for me. He called a separate ambulance for my children.

I thought they were taking me to hell. I would not take the charcoal that they wanted me to take by mouth because I thought they were trying to poison me. Because I wouldn't take the charcoal, they believed I was acting the way I was because I had taken drugs. The doctors put a tube down my nose and forced the charcoal into my stomach.

After several tests, they discovered that I hadn't taken any drugs. They placed me in a wheelchair and took me to a room on the fourth floor of the hospital, which I later found out was the psychiatric ward. I was placed in a room with a bed and a toilet. I didn't know why I was there or what was happening to me. I felt like a caged animal.

The next morning I was placed in another room with a teenager. A young doctor came in and introduced himself.

I was given several medications. One of them was an antipsychotic, Haldol. It made me feel like a zombie. I slurred my speech and moved slowly. Some of the staff were compassionate, but others were critical and unsympathetic.

Many visitors came to see me, which lifted my spirits. My sister came from Provo, and it was good to see her. My husband brought me a beautiful bouquet of baby pink roses, and he told me that he never realized how sick I was and not to worry because we would work it all out together. I realized what a controlled environment I was in when the roses had to be placed in an unbreakable vase.

After much testing, my diagnosis was postpartum psychosis. One in 100,000 women suffers from postpartum psychosis. But my doctor knew someone who had suffered from postpartum psychosis, and he called her to come assist me and give me some counsel on how she was able to overcome her problems. This was a great help to me. I felt that she was one of Heavenly Father's little miracles. She lived about five miles from me, and I hadn't even known her. It was wonderful to have somebody understand just how I felt.

When I was released from the hospital, I became discouraged and depressed. My mind was like a TV that you turn on and all you get is static—on every channel. I couldn't concentrate. The things I had enjoyed before, such as reading and listening to music, now gave me little pleasure because my mind wasn't able to process the words or music. I felt like I had been shot with Novocain. I was numb, and it was hard to do the simplest of tasks.

It was hard for me to go back to church. Many people were cruel and unkind. They would scowl at me and then turn their heads. I later found out that there was a rumor going around the ward that I had been going to throw my children into a reservoir. The truth was that there was no reservoir anywhere near where I was on the mountain.

My psychologist was another one of Heavenly Father's little miracles. He was a wonderful support and counselor to me. But the medications didn't seem to be working. I was on an antidepressant that meant I couldn't eat some foods, such as cheese. I was on Lithium for mood swings. I believe I was still on the Haldol at that time. I still wasn't able to sleep, and my doctor had me try first Benadryl and then Xanax. The Xanax would help me sleep during the day but not at night. I was really getting depressed. I felt like an animal walking through the forest and falling into a trap with dirt all around me and a little ray of light at the top. The ray of light seemed so far away. I wasn't sleeping and my body had just kind of shut down or turned off. I didn't have menstrual periods for months and couldn't even force myself to eat. I lost fifty pounds. I couldn't see any way out.

I had made a pact with my doctor that if I ever became suicidal I would go into the hospital. I called and told him that I would need to go into the hospital because I had become suicidal. I knew the correct way to slit my wrists so that I could die quickly, and I felt tempted to do it.

In the hospital I made some friends among the other patients and the staff. We shared similar problems and I remember their kindness. One time we all told each other what we liked about each other and they said what a friendly and cheerful person I was. Hearing these compliments really helped boost my self-esteem. The other patients were so caring. We discovered that most of us were in nurturing professions. My psychologist in the hospital even told us that one time in his life he had planned suicide, and this made us all feel understood. I had asked the staff to keep any items away from me that I could harm myself with.

When I got home, I was still struggling to do the simplest of tasks, like changing the baby or even putting fish sticks in the oven. My psychologist, who worked for LDS Social Services, took me on as a private patient. He was a godsend. He even took only half the fee, which the insurance paid as full payment. He told me that I was in a bad marital situation, but I would be in a worse situation if I got a divorce. I felt like a failure because I wasn't able to take very good care of my children. But he helped me realize that feeding my children Cheerios for breakfast and peanut butter sandwiches for lunch and putting them into bed in their clothing wouldn't kill them, but not having me in there lives would break their hearts.

My doctor tried hard to find the right combinations of medication for me. He kept having me try different medications to help me come out of my depression. At one time I had to take Thorazine to be able to sleep, but doors opened and new medications came out, and I was finally able to sleep well. A new antidepressant came out, Wellbutrin, which helped with my depression. I no longer have the highs, but I don't have the lows either, which is a modern-day medical miracle. One word of wisdom is this: take the medications your doctor prescribes. My doctor told me that I had been one of the worst patients to take my medications and also the best. For years I have been one of the best and have been well and happy. So be sure to take your medications.

My sister and brother-in-law exemplified the scripture: "And whosoever shall compel thee to go a mile, go with him twain" (Matthew 5:41). My brother-in-law had helped clean my house while I was in the hospital. He and my sister took my six children to Idaho Falls so I could get some rest when I came home from the hospital. They kept them there for two weeks, which helped me greatly. Several other times during the following year they kept the children, especially the youngest ones, with them while the older four were in school. It helped me out. I don't know what I would have done without them. They were marvelous, and I will be eternally grateful for their support.

Not everyone in the ward showed contempt for me. Many followed the scripture "for inasmuch as ye do it unto the least of these, ye do it unto me" (D&C 42:38). My Relief Society president called me every day to see how I was doing. A woman in our ward who had had a nervous breakdown called me every day. I truly appreciated their calls. My dear friend, whom my doctor sent, took my children and me to her house to have lunch on several occasions. She would also drop over little presents she had painted. These acts of kindness were greatly valued.

Mental illness is hard to understand. My psychologist says that people with mental illness are the modern-day lepers. My bishop during this time didn't understand mental illness at all. He felt that all I needed was to be more organized. He felt that I was in control of my faculties when I went up the mountain with my children. He didn't realize that I had gone completely psychotic and was in an imaginary world of my own. Some people refused to talk to me. They wouldn't even look at me when I was near them. They wouldn't let their children play with my children. But I still stayed with the Church. In some ways I felt like my family and I were being treated as lepers. Several of my children went inactive in the Church later in their lives because of the way we were treated at this time. One daughter told me later that after Young Women's meetings others wouldn't even give her a ride home.

More than anything, it hurt me most that our friends and ward members thought what I did on the mountain was my fault, as if it was something I had had control over. They thought I did it on purpose. Only three or four friends didn't blame me.

For a long time I felt great anger towards the bishop, but I have come to realize that we are only human and sometimes err in our thinking. Our Savior stands as our prime example of forgiveness. When he was nailed upon the cross he said, "Father, forgive them; for they know not what they do" (Luke 23:34). It took me a long time to forgive what I felt were the injustices of the situation, but one day almost a year later I was able to turn it over to the Lord and forgive this man, which gave me great peace and joy. "If ye forgive men their trespasses, your heavenly Father will also forgive you: But if ye forgive not men their trespasses, neither will your father forgive your trespasses" (Matthew 6:14–15).

When I started to take my medications regularly and truly forgave, my life started improving greatly. I started selling Avon and became a successful salesperson. This helped me meet some new friends and earn a little extra income. But in the spring of 1990 my psychologist told me that he felt I needed to get a job to help our financial situation. I got a job at a local nursing home and went to school to become a certified nurse's aide. I was busy and relied on my older girls to watch the younger children and take care of things. I couldn't have made it without their help.

Our family went through another shocking experience in January 1992. My husband was diagnosed with colon cancer and had his first surgery. The cancer was removed, and then he had to go through chemo-therapy and radiation. When he completed these treatments, the doctors gave him a clean bill of health. We were grateful for this miracle.

My husband always went in for his cancer blood tests, but in the spring of 1995 he was having severe pain in his abdomen and the doctors discovered cancer again. The doctors operated, but they discovered that cancer had spread throughout his abdominal cavity and closed him back up. He tried chemotherapy again but soon died.

I have found through my experience with mental illness that I have a predisposition for chemical imbalance. My mother had to have shock treatments and also suffered from depression. When I was a patient in treatment at the hospital, we learned the phrase "elephants in the closet." This means that information is often withheld from us that could be beneficial to us if we knew it. I found out after my mother's death that my great-grandfather had drowned himself in a bucket of water. Other family members suffer from depression. My niece, a beautiful and tal-ented mother of four and a bishop's wife, tried to commit suicide two years ago. They didn't have any marital or financial troubles, but the gene pool surfaced again in the life of a family member.

My mental illness was a long and hard ordeal. I always had a strong testimony. I refused to be a leper. I kept going to church and paying my tithing. I feel that I am a better person for having gone through these trials. I feel that I have become more compassionate, less judgmental, and more spiritual because of going through these trials.

My experience on the mountain happened fourteen years ago, and my husband died six years ago. I continue to take an antidepressant (Wellbutrin), an antipsychotic (Geodone), and a sleeping medication. I wouldn't go without my medication. Recently someone in my ward said people in Utah use more prescriptions than anyone else. Later that day the Relief Society president said we shouldn't take medications but rather go to God. I thought, *How sad. They don't know what mental illness is really like.* I don't dare *not* take my medications. If you have a chemical imbalance, there is nothing you can do but take your medicine.

I received many blessings during my mental illness, but there is one blessing that really helped me realize what a great love my Heavenly Father has for each of his children. The blessing stated that the Lord knew me. I was told that Heavenly Father had wept over my trials. I was told how pleased the Lord was with me in how I had treated my parents. This blessing truly helped me comprehend the great love our Heavenly Father has for each and every one of us.

My Son, "A Son of God"?

Doreen L. Christensen

Doreen and her husband, Gordon, are the parents of seven children. They have been married for forty-six years. Doreen serves as a Young Women leader, and her husband is in the bishopric. They have one son who suffers from schizophrenia.

We had just returned from the church, where we had attended sacrament meeting. Our son, James, had been honored at a mission farewell. A member of the stake presidency had spoken and said James was the most prepared missionary he had seen or heard. When James spoke, it was more like the testimony of a returning missionary than one who was just leaving. It was a spiritual occasion. Family, neighbors, and friends were coming and going through our home that Sabbath day. I stood by my son in our front room as the crowd thinned out. James said several things that made me wonder what was going on in his mind. This was one of the first times I really thought something might be wrong. I don't recall what he said, but I remember thinking, *If he really had those feelings, should he be going on this mission?* But he went on his mission anyway. In retrospect I wish I had sought advice at that time.

My husband and I have spent many years in Church service. I have been Relief Society president. My husband has served on the high council and has been a bishop. Professionally he worked as a counselor with teenagers. As a child and a young man, James seemed to do okay. He went to church with us, participated in Scouts, and did well in school. James had the IQ of a genius. In addition to being an exceptional student in school, he was a remarkable musician. His patriarchal blessing seemed so wonderful. It read in part:

> You are a choice son of your Heavenly Father
> and He loves you. . . . You were valiant in the spirit

> world where you sat at the council tables and were among those who approved the plan of salvation as it was presented by your elder brother, Jesus Christ. . . . He has sent you here with a special mission to perform.

Never in our worst dreams did we ever expect to have to deal with what James and his mental illness brought to our home over the next few years. While on his mission he changed. We learned later that the mental illness of schizophrenia often onsets in late adolescence and early adulthood. James was at the prime age for this type of mental illness to begin.

James went on his mission to South America. His first companion would not let him give a discussion for the first month, nor would he allow him to shower, until there was an altercation and he showered anyway, or so James said. James had set an unrealistic goal of baptizing one thousand individuals and felt that if he fasted and prayed enough he would accomplish it. His letters seemed normal until halfway through his mission. Then his handwriting changed, and he didn't seem to be remembering what was happening. We learned later that he would get lost from his companion and quite often proselyted alone. He said his fellow missionaries called him the "crazy" one. We often wanted to call him and find out what was happening, but being obedient to the mission rules, we did not call. His condition worsened. We didn't realize how sick he was until he came home.

On his way home James flew from South America to Florida. At customs he could not find his plane ticket to reboard. His companions left him. (His ticket turned up in Los Angeles with one of his companions.) He called, telling us he had lost his ticket and wanted to walk home, preaching along the way. We paid for another ticket, and he was to get on the next flight home. The plane was grounded by bad weather at Fort Lauderdale, and James became confused. He had few belongings and no coat, and when the police tried to get his name, the only ID he had was his temple recommend. He fought with them, thinking it was wrong for them to see it.

One of the policemen was married to an LDS woman, so he took James to the home of the stake mission president in that area. We were waiting at the Salt Lake airport when a call came from the stake mission president saying that James had serious problems and wanted to know what to do with him. James stayed in the president's home that night, and we wired another ticket. He put James on the plane and informed the stewardesses of James's situation. I shall never forget what I saw when our son emerged from the airplane. His hands were in the pockets of a pair of suit pants that had been hand patched with four or five layers of different fabric, and he wore a tattered white shirt. He looked like a homeless person, not the handsome young man we had sent on a mission. None of the clothes and supplies that we had sent with him came home. He had a carryall that smelled of mold, with nothing in it except a few trinkets that had been given to him. We had sent money for him to buy a handmade guitar. He had no idea of what had happened to the money or any of the equipment he had taken.

Needless to say, I was devastated. We took him to a doctor, and James had his first psychiatric hospitalization.

That was the beginning of a heartbreaking situation that still continues in our lives almost twenty years later. As active members of the Church, my husband and I had somehow believed that something like this could never happen to us. We had family home evening. We attended the temple regularly. We did everything we possibly could to raise a celestial family. We knew that God lived and that the gospel is true. But nothing prepared us for what mental illness brought into our lives. We had always believed that because we were trying to do the right things in our home and follow the guidelines of the Church as best we could, we would be blessed. James's illness did not seem to be a blessing to us, and it was almost more than we could bear. We felt this was not supposed to be happening to us.

After James's first hospitalization, we knew the situation was serious. During this time there were troubles in the Falkland Islands. James said he was the cause of the trouble and had to go and make things right. When we insisted that he see a doctor, he asked us to kneel and pray and we would follow the answer that was received. After we had all prayed, he said he had received his answer. He declared that he was perfectly fine and didn't need any further help. We felt deep within our hearts that he was greatly in need of professional help.

Over the past years, there have been many doctors, medications, treatments, hospitalizations, several attempted suicides, and experiences that have been greatly challenging for the whole family. James's younger brother had difficulty coping with what was happening and turned to drugs. In hindsight, my husband and I feel that we forgot about the other children in the family because all our waking hours and resources were focused on dealing with James. The medications and treatment sometimes helped. One of the biggest problems was that James didn't believe he needed medication and counseling, and he wouldn't take his medication or attend counseling regularly. Things remained chaotic.

James met a girl at the mall and a relationship developed. He started living with her. We talked them into getting married and had a reception for them. They moved to Seattle, where he worked for a little while. One day we got a phone call. James apparently had been watching a TV show on how the *Superman* movie was made. He thought he could fly and tried to fly through the front window of a second story apartment. He cut one of his legs so badly he was hospitalized.

His mental condition worsened after this event. He was placed again in a psychiatric unit, this time in Seattle. My husband and I drove to Seattle to pick him up from the psychiatric unit. He was receiving high doses of a medication we knew he couldn't tolerate. When we went to the hospital, the doctor told us it was unusual for parents to come and get someone in his mental condition. Usually they just left the person and never returned. This hurt me. I had such a love for our son and wanted to do everything possible to help him get better. By now there was no doubt he was severely mentally ill. Although at that time we were still unsure what we should do to help James, we knew that our love for God, our love for his son Jesus Christ, and our love for our son James would not let us abandon him. Doctrine and Covenants 18:10 says, "Remember the worth of souls is great in the sight of God." I knew that James's life had purpose and that he is as important to his Father in Heaven as I am. But in the early years I think I knew this in my head, but I didn't believe it in my heart. Sometimes I was angry at James and what he was doing to our family.

James's wife divorced him, and he moved in with us. Through proper mental health care he did find a combination of medicines that enabled him to function reasonably well for a while. We never got our old son back, but he was better when he took the medicines. In fact, he would get to feeling so good that he felt he didn't need medicine and would quit taking it only to find he really needed it. Each time he resumed his medicine, it seemed to be less effective. This was a difficult time for us. We never knew what was going to happen next. James would be sleeping downstairs and during the night would come to our bedroom to talk to us. He would feel that he had visions and received messages from God. Some of the messages were frightening. He told us that if God told him to, he would have to kill us. He would tell us other strange things.

As we began to learn about schizophrenia, we learned that it was not unusual for those suffering from it to have irrational beliefs associated with religion and Jesus. During those years we slept lightly and kept a baseball bat under the bed for protection. We didn't know what else to do. We tried everything. He was given blessings. We talked to our priesthood leaders. We went to the local community mental health clinic. We took him to the hospital. We called the police. He was hospitalized several more times. We kept having the hope that "this time" he was going to be cured, and our son would return. But he was never cured. Things went on in the same way.

Over the years, I learned to dread the phone ringing. Who would it be this time? Would it be the police? Would it be the hospital? Would it be James in another crisis situation? Or would it be the mortuary? And when times were really bad, I admit I hoped in some ways it would be the mortuary and perhaps he would be dead. I felt in some strange way then all this madness would end if he were dead. But the mortuary never called.

The bottom line was I had to learn to endure. This was something I had to learn to deal with and accept. As much as I hated the thought, the real challenge wasn't really how I dealt with James—he basically stayed the same (or gradually got worse) no matter what we tried to do to help. The real question was, could I hang in there, day after day, month after month, and year after year? Could I still believe in God when all of this was over? Would I have a testimony of the gospel the day James was buried?

Some days are more difficult than others. Scriptures about enduring to the end became a meaningful part of my life. Scriptures such as 3 Nephi 27:6—"And whoso taketh upon him my name, and endureth to the end, that same shall be saved at the last day"—were sometimes the only thing I had to hang on to. I knew that somewhere inside me, I just had to endure. I couldn't give up.

Whatever the reason, treatments didn't work well for James. We met some families along the way in which the medications did wonders for their children. Their schizophrenic child could actually hold a job, go to church, and be a responsible parent. That was not true for James. Nothing seemed to work for long. During those years I learned I had to take care of myself so that I would have enough resources to help James. I made sure I had my personal time to pray, to read, and to live.

He met a young woman, and they wanted to get married. He had been going to church and had renewed his temple-worthy status, and so they planned a temple marriage. We met with the young woman and her parents to try to discourage them because of his mental illness. We told the girl and her parents about all the problems James had, but they felt that through faith and prayer he could be healed. They were married, and after a short while James's wife began to realize the seriousness of his problems. She became frustrated when she couldn't figure out why she didn't have enough faith for him to be healed and yet she kept feeling that he would be cured. They have two daughters, who are brilliant like their dad. James tried to take his life several more times after he entered his second marriage.

James had reached a point in his life when he had no friends or worldly possessions. He couldn't hold a job. He had become so obnoxious, contentious, and at times dangerous that his wife and we had to forbid him to come to our homes unless he would behave in an acceptable manner. There were no resources left for him. The community mental health center seemed unconcerned about our son, and we didn't know what else to do but to protect ourselves from him by forbidding him to come around. These were hard times. We wondered where he was and what was happening to him. All I could do is pray for him and hope. During this time he hitchhiked to Mesquite and Las Vegas only to call us to come and get him. We told him he would have to find his own way back. When he got to his wife's home, his feet were bleeding and his legs were swollen black and green. The doctor thought he might have gangrene, so his wife let him live with her for a short time. At this time James was so angry with his father and me that he told us to not come to his home until we were invited.

Not long afterward he called me. In the spring of 1998 he asked me if I would come and talk to him. He welcomed me to his apartment and asked me to sit at the small kitchen table across from him. He talked for a while, telling me of his plans. I was quite amazed at his sensibility. He seemed normal. Then he asked me if I would believe what he was going to tell me. He said that he was Jesus, the son of God. He had a special work to do, and he asked me if I believed him. I told him he wasn't the God I believed in and worshipped. He started getting upset. He had been trying for years to get us to believe that he was deity. As I tried to conduct a limited conversation, he became angrier and finally stood, pointed to the door, and told me to leave and never come back. I left. Over the years we have had many conversations that have ended in the same way.

In the summer of 1998 James had a heart attack. I was with him early in the morning when he was having difficulty breathing and said he was going to die. I believed he might die this time. He was rushed to the emergency room and was revived. He had started smoking again, and the smoke was keeping him from getting the oxygen he needed. He refused to quit smoking or to have proper medical procedures carried out.

After experiencing such serious health problems, he has gradually seemed to mellow. He is depressed. His physical health is poor. His mental health is the same. The doctors have told us that he has only a year or two left to live.

His great musical talents are about gone, but he continues to write wonderful poetry. He can't sing as well as he used to. His guitar is in the pawnshop most of the time. His other musical equipment has been gone for years. The sparkle in his eye is gone too. Probably the greatest loss is that of his testimony and understanding of the gospel. He doesn't seem to understand anything that normal people understand. He accuses us of not loving him. After almost twenty years, we wait. We wait for that one last phone call. My heart aches when I think of James and what mental illness has done to him.

As I have gone through various experiences, emotions, trials, and heartaches for these many years, I have experienced much growth. I had to. I either had to grow and deal with it or be swallowed up with the grief and pain. The gospel of Jesus Christ has given me the purpose and desire to keep going and finish this race. At first the difficulty was almost more than I could stand. As years passed, however, I learned to accept the chronic nature of James's mental illness and that he was not going to be "cured" in this lifetime. That truth seemed unbearable at first, but after a while I came to believe it. I quit believing that every time I saw any improvement that this would be the time he would be cured. I realized that I had to live with myself, my husband, my other children, my grandchildren, and James and his mental illness.

I think back to the time at the kitchen table with James when he asked me over to talk. I couldn't see it then, but I'm beginning to see it now. The words from one of the songs from *Les Miserables* come to my mind. The words "To love another person is to see the face of God." Could I see the "face of God" sitting across from me? Everyone could see James's mental illness. That was easy. The small apartment. Another broken marriage. Poor physical health. No job. Bizarre thinking. The list goes on and on. But could I see the Father and his elder brother Jesus in James's face? Could I look beyond the scars of mental illness and see James's real worth? His real heart? In 1 Samuel 16:3–7, we are told of Samuel choosing a king. Verse 7 reads: "But the Lord said unto Samuel, look not on his countenance, or on the height of his stature; because I have refused him: for the Lord seeth not as man seeth; for man looketh on the outward appearance, but the Lord looketh on the heart."

I think I catch a glimpse now and then of what this is all about. I don't have all the answers. But I believe this trial is not about James and the horror of schizophrenia. It's about me. It's about me, regardless of what I've done or haven't done over the many years. The question is, can I love him one more day? Can I look through his mental illness and see the face of God? I know that someday James will be in a better world and this terrible condition will be gone. The resurrection will fix that chemical imbalance in James's brain. I can hardly wait for the time my son and I can talk, on the other side of the veil. Oh, the stories we will share! I'm not quite sure how it will all end up, but somehow I just believe James will be part of my eternal family. That I, by enduring to the end, will be worthy of being his mother, once again.

The scriptures have been a guide and also a source of strength, even survival, during the hard times. Maybe James has been right all these years. I'm believing more and more that he is a "son of God," not his son Jesus, but his son James. Maybe it's true—"my son, a son of God!" Imagine that. I'm not there yet, but maybe the statement "my boy, a son of God" is with an exclamation point and not a question mark.

James recently wrote me a poem:

Dear Mom,

For all the tears you wiped away
For making nighttime seem like day
For keeping me an upright kid
For all the puzzles that we did

For helping me to see the light
For changing every wrong to right
For softly singing lullabies
For answering my endless "whys"

For all these things and countless more
You kept me going, made me soar
And now in tribute, mother dear
Please let me whisper in your ear

Three words that tell the story true
My mother dear, how I love you!

EATING DISORDERS

The two most common eating disorders are anorexia nervosa and bulimia nervosa. With eating disorders the normal eating habits become disrupted and polarized. In some eating disorders like anorexia, the person ceases to eat at all, while in others like bulimia, the person may binge-eat, consuming extremely large amounts of food. Another common factor related to eating disorders is a distorted body image. The person perceives herself as having some physical defect, such as being overweight, when in fact she is not.

Symptoms

Anorexia Nervosa

- Extreme weight loss and believing that one is fat despite excessive thinness are key features of anorexia.

- Skips meals, takes tiny portions, will not eat in front of others, or eats in ritualistic ways.

- Always has an excuse not to eat.

- Will only eat a few "safe," low-calorie, low-fat foods.

- Loses hair, looks pale or malnourished, wears baggy clothes to hide thinness.

- Loses weight yet fears obesity and complains of being fat despite excessive thinness.

- Detests all or specific parts of the body, insists she or he cannot feel good about self unless thin.

- Exercises excessively and compulsively.

- Holds to rigid, perfectionist standards for self and others.

- Withdraws into self and feelings, becoming socially isolated.

- Has trouble talking about feelings, especially anger.

Bulimia Nervosa

- Regularly binge-eats and then attempts to prevent gaining weight from the binge through purging (vomiting, abusing laxatives, exercising excessively).

- Binges, usually in secret, and empties cupboards and refrigerator.

- Buys "binge food" (usually junk food or food high in calories, carbohydrates, and sugar).

- Leaves clues that suggest discovery is desired: empty food packages, foul-smelling bathrooms, running water to cover sounds of vomiting, use of breath fresheners, poorly hidden containers of vomit.

- Uses laxatives, diet pills, water pills, or "natural" products to promote weight loss.

- Abuses alcohol or street drugs to deaden appetite or escape emotional pain.

- Displays a lack of impulse control that can lead to rash and regrettable decisions about sex, money, commitments, careers, and so forth.

He Knows You Are There

Heather Anderson

Heather is married to Jeff. She tells the story of coping with her eating disorder.

I am the youngest of six children. My family was considered the perfect family in the LDS community. We attended church every Sunday, sitting on the first row with our hair done, looking good, sitting up straight. From our outside appearance, we did look like the perfect family. My parents were prominent people in the community. Both held high-profile job positions and were known by many. So, from a young age, we were told not to do anything wrong to draw attention to ourselves because it would make our parents look bad.

While our family appeared perfect the truth was that something horrible was happening in our house. I had a brother who was about four years older than me. He was sexually abusing me. I was also raped by one of his friends. The abuse from my brother went on for many, many years.

One day, in eighth grade, I was in my last class of the day, math. I really couldn't concentrate or focus on anything going on that day because I knew in my heart that this could not go on any longer. I knew that something had to be done. I felt so ugly, so used, and so betrayed. I couldn't tell my parents what was happening. I wasn't stupid. I knew that I would be taken out of the house if I did. I couldn't tell anybody at school. I couldn't tell any of the Young Women leaders because my mom was my leader at the time. I also didn't want to bring that type of shame on my parents.

I remember sitting on the bus and thinking there was only one option for me. I went home from school. I took out of the medicine cabinet an entire year's supply of Phenobarbital, which my brother took for epilepsy, plus some other medicines. I color-coordinated them all nicely on the counter, and I swallowed them all. The next thing I remember was my mom holding me in her arms as they rushed me to the hospital. My next memory after that was three and a half weeks later. I had been in a coma for that long.

My sisters told me that they gathered my family around and said, "We don't know if she'll live. If she does live, we don't know what extensive damage she has done to her brain. And so we're just going to have to wait and see." My parents and my family waited by my side for those weeks. And then one day, I just woke up. I looked around and wondered what was going on. Many therapists came to my bedside to try to learn why I did what I did. One in particular stands out. This doctor came in, pulled a chair next to my bed, and said, "I am 'the doctor' of Utah Valley Hospital. I am going to decide today whether you are going to go home with your parents or if you are going to a lock-up unit. So, I want you to be honest with me and tell me why you did what you did."

I looked at this man I didn't know. I was a little fourteen-year-old girl who was scared of men. I lied to him. I told him I had a boyfriend who was pressuring me to have sex and I didn't want to. I said that he broke up with me, and I was so totally devastated that I could no longer go on living. I remember him patting my leg and saying, "Now, doesn't that feel good to talk about it? I'll let you go home with your parents now." Right then I made the conscious decision that I could trust no one.

So we went home, and my life proceeded as normal, or at least the normal that I knew. My family never talked about my attempt on my life. My dad made it clear that we were never to talk about it. I felt, once again, that I was a failure and that I couldn't do anything right. I got into high school and started dating a boy. He was nice to everybody but me. He would tell me on a daily basis that I was lucky that he was dating me because I was probably the ugliest girl in Utah County. He would hit me if I wouldn't do something he wanted me to do. The make-up part of all of that was great, however. He would bring me roses and jewelry.

I had been taught always to forgive. So I would forgive and forget. It came time for this young man to serve a mission, and he went. But every day at 3 P.M. he would call me from his mission to make sure I was home. This happened my entire senior year of school. This guy was thousands of miles away, and yet, I was so terrified of him that I would run home every day to make sure I got that phone call. I graduated from high school, and he was sent home from his mission, for obvious reasons. We were at the point in our relationship that we were going to get married. I thought that if we went through the temple the hurtful words and fists would stop.

During this time I was working as a waitress. I loved my boss, even though he was much older than I was. He was the nicest guy. I had never known that guys came that way. I would say to myself, "Oh, I'd give my right arm to go out with this guy." And yet, I was nearly engaged to this other guy. Finally, one day this man came up to me and said, "Hey, Heather, what are you doing this Thursday night?" I about died. I said, "Nothing." He said, "Do you want to go out?" I agreed. We went out and have been together ever since, fourteen years now. He became my husband.

There is something important that you need to know about my husband. When he dated me and proposed, he knew nothing about my background. I made sure of it! Because he really did, from all appearances, come from a perfect family. It was hard for me to open up to him. I thought that if he knew who I really was and if he saw what I had gone through, he wouldn't want me. I kept everything a secret.

I remember the day we got married at the Salt Lake Temple. We were the first to be married that morning, so we had to be there at five. I was sitting in the celestial room, and all of the little old ladies were walking around making sure I was okay. This was supposed to be the best day of my life. But I just sat there in the celestial room thinking, *I am not worthy to be here. Heavenly Father hates me. Look what I've done with my life.* My husband was sitting next to me, just beaming. I was too big of a chicken to say anything. I went through the marriage ceremony and reception with a smile on my face. It wasn't long after that when I started my eating disorder.

I started my eating disorder because I had such horrible feelings about myself, about everything around me, and about my lies. I just couldn't take it any more. My eating disorder gave me something else to think about. It started very, very slowly for me. I would start by skipping breakfast, and then lunch, and then dinner. Weeks would go by without my eating. Sometimes I could go two to two and a half weeks without eating anything solid except a potato chip a day and sometimes a soda. That seemed to get me through. It just kept getting worse and worse.

I worked at a doctor's office, which my father-in-law owned. I would go to work with my clothes and lab coats hanging off me and my belts wrapped around my waist. I looked gray, and my hair was actually falling out. I remember when I went into a room to draw a patient's blood. I inserted the needle into the patient's arm and I passed out. Of course she freaked out because there was blood going everywhere. The doctors rushed in and took care of her and then they picked me up. They took me into their office, sat me down, and said, "Heather, we know something is wrong with you. We are going to give you an ultimatum." I thought, you don't give Heather Anderson an ultimatum. But I said, "Okay, what is it?" They said, "Either you get help, or you're fired." Keep in mind that my father-in-law was sitting in this room with me. I told them that I would get help on one condition—nobody could tell Jeff, my husband. Nobody else could know, not my mother-in-law, not anybody! They agreed.

I got in touch with a therapist. I made an appointment for the evening for a few reasons: First, so that the receptionist would know only a name, not a face. Second, because my husband worked nights, so he wouldn't know where I was going. And third, because I didn't want anybody that was driving down the street to see me go into a therapist's office. That is how paranoid I was. I remember sitting on his couch and him saying, "So do you want to tell me why you are here?" I told him I didn't know why I was there. I had no problems and besides, all men are jerks. I proceeded to go off on him and he just politely listened to me for an hour. After the hour was up, he said, "Well, I think maybe we have a problem. I would like to invite you back." I replied, "There is no way I am setting foot in this office again." He simply nodded and agreed.

But I went back. I kept going back until he gained my trust enough for me to finally tell him about my abuse. He worked through that with me for a long time before it was time for me to tell Jeff. I remember that night going home. I was driving home thinking that we didn't have any children and Jeff could leave me so easily. But I had promised that I would do this. I went into the house. Jeff was, ironically, making dinner for himself. He could tell that something was wrong, so he inquired. I stood firm and really strong because if he was going to hit me, I was not going to fall. I said, "Listen, this is what's been going on in our marriage and this is what's been going on in my life." I laid it all out for him, and then I just stood there. I actually expected him to start yelling at me.

But he didn't. He dropped to his knees, held onto my legs, and said, "Heather, I married you for time and eternity. I'm not leaving you. There is no way you are getting rid of me that easily." I just looked at the sky and thought, *Wow, nobody has ever cried for me before.* I didn't know what to do.

Little did Jeff know that his life would get much worse. Sometimes he would come home from work and the doors would be locked because I couldn't handle his coming into the house and being so supportive. I just couldn't handle it. He would patiently sit on the front porch until I unlocked the front door. He would simply ask if I wanted him to make me some soup. He would go through the whole thing—sitting me down, spoon-feeding me soup. Sometimes after one bite, I would say, "Okay, that's all I can do. That's all I can do." He would reply, "That's okay, you did great! We'll try again tomorrow." He was actually watching me die, but he never once said a negative word to me.

Then I got pregnant with our son. I was sick, but I actually really did want to eat for him. I would put food into my body, but my body had been without food for so long that it didn't know what to do with it. So I would automatically throw it right back up. Eventually I had to go into the hospital three times a day for IV therapy for breakfast, lunch, and dinner just to sustain his life. He was born in his eighth month because of my eating disorder. He weighed four pounds, but he was perfect. I got to take him home three days later.

My eating disorder, however, continued down the road of destruction. It came to a point in our lives where Jeff and my therapist said that I needed to be an in-patient somewhere. There was no place to put me except Utah Valley Hospital. I was admitted. I was there for a week and was a model patient. I did all my food eating, percentages of food, everything that I was asked to do. I said all the right things at group and individual therapy. I did everything right. One night I called Jeff and said, "If you don't get me out of here tomorrow, I will serve you divorce papers." I was out the next day. I just couldn't handle it. I wasn't ready to get better. I wanted to hang onto my eating disorder. I didn't want somebody telling me that I needed to give that up.

I continued down my road of destruction when I got pregnant the second time.

But this time when I got pregnant I weighed eighty-four pounds. If I thought my first pregnancy was bad, the second was a multitude worse. They actually ended up putting a central line into my heart, and I carried around a backpack of food for my daughter. When I was seven months pregnant, the doctor put me on the scale. I weighed 117 pounds. He said, "What are you doing?" I didn't know what to say to him. Alex was born in her eighth month, weighing five pounds. She, too, was perfect and beautiful. The nurses called her Peanut. Sometimes I would look at myself, look at her, and then look back at myself. I would think to myself, "She did this to me. She made me fat. She made me look the way I do." So for about the first three months of Alex's life, I would only hold her for pictures. I wouldn't feed her. I didn't want to have anything to do with her. Jeff was her mother. You should see Alex today. She is my ten-year-old, my best friend, my little sidekick.

Then came a time when I really crashed and burned. We had just built a house in Pleasant Grove. I decided that I wasn't going to live there anymore. I wasn't going to be a member of the Mormon church anymore because everybody was so condescending. They looked at me, and I knew they were talking about me behind my back. I wanted to move. I wanted to go where nobody knew me. So Jeff put a "for sale" sign on the house we had just built. We moved to another area.

I wasn't going to church at that time. Jeff tried to reason with me about going to church in the new area. "Let's just go to sacrament meeting. We will sit in the very back. We will go in after the opening song, and we will leave before the closing song." I made him promise that that is what would happen. He promised. I agreed to go. We sat in the very back. As I sat there, I knew the bishop was looking right at me the entire time. I tried to hide behind people's heads, but I knew he was looking at me. When the closing song started, Jeff did not move. He was not going to get up. I was looking at him. He knew I wasn't going to get up by myself and walk out. He just sat there and sang the closing song. After sacrament meeting was over, the bishop was standing right there in front of us. He welcomed us to the ward and expressed his gratitude for our being there. He asked when he could come visit us. I wasn't going to tell him no. I knew how this whole thing went. I am a polite person, so I agreed that he could come to our home. Everything was good. The members were very nice.

I eventually got the dreaded call from the bishop. He said that he needed to come over and speak to me. I turned to Jeff and said, "It better be the nursery. It better be the nursery." The bishop came and said, "We would like to extend a calling to you. Would you be the second counselor in the Relief Society presidency?" I started laughing. I said, "First of all, don't you have to be like forty to be in the Relief Society presidency? And second of all, do you even know who I am and what I'm all about?" He said, "Listen, Heather, this calling is not from me. This calling is from the Lord. And if you want to turn it down, you can turn it down. But it is a calling from the Lord."

How could I turn it down? I just couldn't. So I accepted the calling. Except for having to plan a fabulous party once a month, it was the best calling I've ever had! The women in that ward rallied around me and accepted me for who I was. They will never know how much they helped to heal my heart.

I continued to get better as I started reading my scriptures and saying my prayers. I started going to therapy more often. I started to eat. But in this entire process, I had to relearn how to do everything. It wasn't easy. I couldn't just sit down and eat a sandwich. That's not how it worked. I had to go through the whole process of learning what hunger pains were. When my stomach started to hurt, I'd say, "Jeff, my stomach hurts." He would tell me that I was hungry and that those were hunger pains. I had lost the sensation of hunger. So, in the middle of the night, when I woke up with hunger pains, I would tell my husband that I was hungry. He would run to the store and bring me back a subway sandwich because it was one of my "safe foods." I could take a bite, swallow it, and learn to take another bite. Finally, my life progressed to the point where I no longer spat out my saliva in the shower because I knew my saliva was going to make me fat. Once I started working on my inside feelings of who I really was and what I wanted to be, my eating disorder went away.

One night I had a dream. In this dream I was wearing all white and my two children, Mitchell and Alex, were standing next to me. They were wearing all white also. I was carrying an urn. We were just walking. Everything was so peaceful and beautiful. We weren't talking, but Mitchell, Alex, and I were communicating. I couldn't see anything, but somebody said, "Please come to me." So we continued walking.

Finally, we stopped. In my mind a voice said to me, "Please give me your burdens. I've been watching you, and crying for you, and I love you." I had a huge smile on my face in my dream. I handed over the urn, turned around, and walked away with Mitchell and Alex. When I woke up the next morning, I remember thinking that I would never ever forget that my Heavenly Father loves me. He's been crying for me. He knows who I am. I don't think there had ever been a time in my life when I was sitting in Primary and the kids were singing "I am a Child of God" that I really heard that song. I, Heather Anderson, of Lindon, Utah, am a child of God! Heavenly Father loves me for all of my faults and for all of my good. He knows that he sent me here, and he knew that it would be hard. I accepted the challenges that I have here on earth. And I can honestly say that overcoming my eating disorder has made me a better person.

About four years ago, my mother passed away. She and I had never had a very good relationship. I would lie in her bed with her and say, "Mom, do you love me?" She always replied, "Yes." But that wasn't enough for me. I wanted her to express her love for me. I needed her to tell me all of the great things that she thought of me, because she had never really done that my whole life. But then she died. I know in my heart that my mom needed to go into the next life to understand me, to understand the problems that I have, to understand who I am. Now I know for a surety that she loves me.

We are all human. We all make mistakes. If someone were to tell me that my eating disorder was about vanity (which I know a lot of people think it is), that I wanted to look like a supermodel, I would just want to die. I would go days without looking at myself in the mirror because I couldn't stand what I saw. I wanted to hide. I wanted to fade away. I didn't want anybody to see me.

If you know somebody who has an eating disorder, please do not judge him or her because you think that the person wants to look like a supermodel or to be this or that. Please don't. The emotional scars that we carry in our hearts are deep and they are big. Just because we aren't sharing them with you doesn't mean that we don't have them. Just because we look like a little, skinny, perfect person on the outside, please don't judge us. The baggage that we carry around is huge! Say to us that you love us. Just like Heavenly Father would say that he loves us. Go to your Heavenly Father in prayer and ask him to help you in all that you go through. He is there for you, just as he is for me.

Hope and Recovery

Emma Lou Thayne

Emma Lou Thayne is a writer and poet. She and her husband, Melvin, have five daughters, one of whom has suffered from bipolar disorder, bulimia, and anorexia. Emma Lou and her daughter Becky Markosian are the authors of the book *Hope and Recovery: A Mother-Daughter Story about Anorexia Nervosa, Bulimia, and Manic Depression.*

A TV teaser for the ten o'clock news: Which Salt Lake City high school is labeled Bulimia High? Later on prime time, a class of slim seventeen-year-olds does aerobic exercises between bingeing and throwing up.

A father keeps count of calories and fat grams for his family by reading labels at the table and watching every morsel eaten by his kids—even his wife—who rebel and spend money in secret on candy and ice cream or beer.

Athletes try to improve their skills with diet pills for energy and then need sleeping pills for a decent night's sleep.

A mother with a history of depression fights for her life every day as the days fade into drudgery and drudgery into despair and she doesn't dare admit she needs professional help.

Worst of all, high school classmates sing at the funeral of a beloved eighteen-year-old friend who decides not to take his prescribed anti-depressant and commits suicide rather than face graduation.

While more than a third of the world goes hungry, food has become a wily enemy to both affluent and not-so-affluent Americans. How to eat less? How to get rid of the more that has been eaten?

At the same time, millions face every day being either clinically depressed, even suicidal, or maniacally out of control.

The stigma of admitting to mental illness or an eating disorder is often too great to risk telling anyone, let alone trying to find help. Until the past decade, what ordinary person knew much about either disease? Now hardly anyone has not heard of both. But unfortunately, the stigma remains. For the December 29, 2001, issue of the *Church News,* which emphasized peace, the editor, not knowing about our family's history of mental illness, asked me to write about penning the words to the Church hymn "Where Can I Turn for Peace?" It was not hard to write those lyrics.

The spring of 1970 had not been a happy time. The eldest of our five daughters was at nineteen struggling with what we'd never heard of—manic depression/bipolar disease, bulimia, and anorexia. The beautiful girl who had grown up enjoying school, friends, boyfriends, swimming, and water skiing had become obsessed with dieting, and when the boy she sent on a mission didn't write, she fell into a depression unlike anything we could comprehend.

Then, away at college, she became manic and had to come home to be hospitalized. When could she return to herself? To her promising life? In and out of hospitals, through baffling efforts at continuing school, as she fought for her very life through misery and desperation, she and I never lost touch. I have said that a mother is about as happy as her least happy child. Even with other parts of our lives going well, for our family the three years of her healing were the bleakest time I had ever known.

In the midst of this time came June conference. Our Laurel committee of the YWMIA General Board was planning a program for thousands of MIA teachers from across the country. Joleen Meredith had written music to my lyrics for other songs, but on the Saturday morning before the conference, we discussed needing a finale. Why not a hymn? I promised to call back and went to my desk in the storage room in the basement among the clotheslines, sleeping bags, and Christmas decorations.

Sitting at my makeshift desk, I asked on paper what I had implored — how many times? —

Where can I turn for peace?
Where is my solace?
Where in my need to know,
Where can I run?
When with a wounded heart, anger, or malice,
I draw myself apart, searching my soul?

Three verses of a poem found their way to the page, voicing my anguish and providing the answer I carried in my heart:

Where, when my aching grows,
Where, when I languish,
Where, in my need to know,
Where can I run?
Where is the quiet hand to calm my anguish?
Who, who can understand?
He, only one.

He answers privately,
Reaches my reaching
In my Gethsemane, Savior and friend.
Gentle the peace he finds
For my beseeching.
Constant He is and kind,
Love without end.

I called Joleen. She had a history of depression in her family, so she understood every word I'd written. She sat at her piano, and as I read a line, she composed a line. By noon we had our hymn. It disappeared after the program only to resurface in the 1985 LDS hymnbook.

We had sought professional help for Becky and found it in a superb doctor and a newfound medical miracle, a simple salt, lithium, that restored her chemical imbalance. She would need it for the rest of her life, except when she was pregnant with her three sons. But it was love from her future husband and the peace expressed in the hymn that provided the ultimate healing for Becky.

The search for inner peace is universal. Who of us does not face grieving, loss, anger, illness, hopelessness? The aching knows no boundaries, age, station, or language. Once my doctor brother, Homer Warner, on a medical mission with his wife, Kay, called me from an island off of Africa to say, "Hello, Lou. I'm homesick for you. We just heard your hymn sung by a wonderful Black chorus in Portuguese!"

I still cannot hear the hymn without gratitude and hope behind my tears. Only last week when I was speaking at a Relief Society gathering in the Lion House, I felt as if I were hearing it for the first time as twenty-five little violinists played Joleen's music right in the midst of their Christmas carols. And most profound of all, at the memorial in the Tabernacle following September 11, 2001, as war clouds gathered, the hymn encompassed for me both the private and the universal as the choir pleaded for the peace that passes understanding, the peace which he, only One, can offer. That he answers I can testify even more fervently than thirty-one years ago when the hymn so inconspicuously began its life. ("Search for Inner Peace Is Universal," *Church News*, 29 December 2001, 5)

My daughter Becky was thirty-seven when she and I listened to a mother talk of the death of her bright, beautiful, far-from-fat sixteen-year-old daughter who had taken baking soda to make throwing up easier. How much soda, doctors could only guess. But it swelled in her intestine and killed her. Listening, Becky broke down, and I shivered with remembering.

As a girl that age, Becky had done equally dangerous and compulsive things to purge her of her most intolerable torment—weighing more than 105 pounds. With her body build, doctors said a more reasonable weight would be more like 115. But reason had nothing to do with her outrageous dieting and the real threat of death. In fact, during her times of depression, suicide had been part of her thinking. Her sickness was a chemical imbalance, manic depression—now called more often bipolar disease—and bulimia-anorexia. In what order they took over her system and how they influenced each other, no one yet seems able to understand. Each was conquered in its own time, but the bulimia took the longest to leave. It was what almost killed her.

Never have I felt less able, more panicky than when Becky's disease, so out of control, controlled every moment of my mothering—mothering that until then had seemed so easy and satisfying.

As parents, Mel and I knew the guilt and torment of feeling somehow responsible for something we had pathetically little knowledge of or ability to make better. All we could do was what we could, and sometimes that seemed painfully feeble in dealing with what then inundated and threatened the peace in all of our lives.

Even without understanding her problem, most people understood enough that they were wonderful support. From others, Becky had to endure rumors and sometimes a medieval sense of mental or emotional illness. A well-meaning Church official, kind and sincere, offered to give Becky a blessing to get rid of her "evil spirits."

Fourteen years later, after working in the Young Women program, Becky learned of a number of girls who were captive to what she had survived. That summer, she called me and said, "Mom, I can help. I've worked with some of these girls and they've listened to me—we've become friends. You remember I talked to two different girls about getting some help? Going to the hospital? Well, they're each doing better, but they're still battling the terrible addiction. And their mothers have called—they're the ones who suffer. The whole family suffers. What if we wrote my story, the two of us? What if it might do some good? What if we could give them some hope?"

Any power in the universe knows—Becky had to know—that from that hopeless pit, her coming back has colored my life—all of our lives— with a happiness that has pervaded many years since. What if even one other person could find some rescue in knowing that she was not alone, that it had happened to Becky and to me?

Becky, now nearly age fifty, knows she is someone who deserves a good life and good health in a well body. "Mom, in all these years, in the good times and the hard ones, I've never been tempted to go back to that horrible habit. That's why I never get over being grateful for you now."

I do know. I feel the raging gratitude too. And anger as the disease of wanting to be thin claims more and more unwary victims. I can blame advertisers and movies, peer pressure and TV imaging. I can blame ignorance and a universal hunger for popularity. I can deplore the effects of parental expectation and sibling rivalries. I can despair at a generation used to instant gratification where the shape of a body is the shape of self or group approval. I can grieve that often depression accompanies or precipitates the loss of self or even a reason to live, when dieting becomes the most important thing in a day.

Becky got better. And so did I.

I did believe in her, but that would never have been enough. It took three years of medical and psychiatric help to retune her body and mind. And the miracle that was the gentle help of Paul, the boy who loved her and became her husband and the father of her three sons and is now grandfather to a baby boy. It took Becky's own courage and tenacity and inner strength.

For those three years, not only nineteen-year-old Becky but also our whole family rode the scary roller coaster of manic depression and bulimia toward rescue. That she got well is the giant blessing in our lives. Like so many thousands of others, ours is a story of desperation and anger—and for us—of love and hope and faith.

AVAILABLE RESOURCES

A combination of resources including medication, education, personal effort, professional help and support from family and Church members helps individuals with mental illness in recovery.

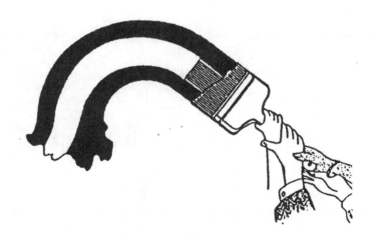

A Holistic Approach to Mental Health

Dr. Jane P. Merrill

Jane P. Merrill is a professional health and weight-control counselor who owned and operated three health and weight-control centers in Idaho. The coauthor of two books, she has presented seminars throughout the United States and Canada. Jane and her husband, Jay, are the parents of six children. She shares principles of healthy living that are particularly beneficial to those experiencing negative normal emotions. The positive-living principles discussed are also helpful in dealing with mental illnesses when used conjointly with professional resources.

President Ezra Taft Benson said, "We live in an age when, as the Lord foretold, men's hearts are failing them not only physically but in spirit. Many are giving up heart for the battle of life. . . . As the showdown between good and evil approaches with its accompanying trials and tribulations, Satan is increasingly striving to overcome the Saints with despair, discouragement, despondency, and depression. Yet, of all people, we as Latter-day Saints should be the most optimistic" (in *Hope* [Salt Lake City: Deseret Book, 1994], 1). Although these conditions can be serious and community resources may be necessary, you can do much to help yourself. Even those with the most serious mental illness can do *some* things to help themselves. Following are some invaluable guidelines for those with mental illness and their families.

Is Your Life in Balance?

A life that gets out of balance is much like a car tire that's out of balance. It makes the car's performance rough and unsafe, even hazardous. It affects other parts of the car, and they may start falling apart. When your life is out of balance, the same thing happens to your mind and body. In contrast, balanced tires help give a smooth, comfortable, safe ride. So it is with life. Living a balanced lifestyle will dramatically improve your ride through life and should form the foundation of any treatment program.

Take Responsibility

Good health is basically a do-it-yourself project. Others can help, but ultimately you must take responsibility and make positive behavioral changes. Changing your lifestyle can produce amazing results in a relatively short time. Take responsibility for your own health by following this safe, easy-to follow program which incorporates *positive living, regular exercise,* and *good nutrition.* This powerful combination offers many benefits, including consistent feelings of well-being, increased mental alertness, natural relaxation, stress control, greater self-confidence, and weight control. Recovery from emotional distress is faster and more permanent as you program your body to release its own antidepressants by living this proven, effective lifestyle. *The principles presented here should be used in addition to, not in place of, conventional professional treatment.*

Positive Thinking

Positive living is gospel living—nourishing the body through prayer, uplifting music, scripture study, church attendance, love and forgiveness, and service to others. God works through positive thoughts, feelings, and actions, all of which help stimulate the production of your body's own mood elevators. The adversary can enter through negative thoughts and emotions such as anger, fear and anxiety.

You can create misery and physical illness in your life by focusing on these negative thoughts and feelings. President Ezra Taft Benson warned, "There are times when you simply have to righteously hang on and outlast the devil until his depressive spirit leaves you" ("Do Not Despair," *Ensign,* November 1974, 65). No matter how dark your mood, when experiencing a negative *normal emotion,* hope is shining brightly for you, and you can and will get some help through positive living. When dealing with a *mental illness,* however, using outside resources in addition to positive-living principles, is necessary.

What Are You Feeding Your Mind?

You can reprogram yourself to some degree by changing your mental attitude. Be positive about every challenge life offers you. Eliminate negative thinking. Replace negative thoughts with constructive, uplifting ambitions and goals. Make a conscious decision to be positive and successful as you strive to fill the measure of your own creation. Repeat positive affirmations. Here are a few to get you started:

- "Every day in every way I'm getting better and better and better."

- "I can do all things through Christ who strengtheneth me" (Philippians 4:13).

- "I feel my Savior's love."

Peaceful thoughts and feelings, as well as good music, are natural mood elevators.

Pray Often

President Spencer W. Kimball said, "Extra needs require extra prayers" ("We Need a Listening Ear," *Ensign,* November 1979, 4). This quotation has graced our home for many years and is a constant source of motivation and strength. Never underestimate the power of prayer. God knows and loves you. He wants to help you. Pray about your problems. Pour out your heart in humble prayer and plead, "Father, please help me." Don't just focus on your problems; focus on finding the *solutions* to your problems.

Answers Will Come

Answers will come through other people, through good books (particularly the scriptures), through circumstances, and especially as the still, small voice of the Spirit speaks to your heart. Your patriarchal blessing as well as priesthood blessings can be powerful sources of guidance and comfort. Answers will come in the Lord's own time and in his own way, but you must do your part. Sometimes the answer is receiving just enough strength to make it through one more day. The old adage "Pray as if everything depends on the Lord; work as if everything depends on you" holds true. Remember, *God is in the business of helping you help yourself!* This may include turning to those in the professional community who are there to help you.

Regular Exercise

Activate nature's tranquilizer. Regular exercise is an excellent natural remedy for many types of stress. It has been called the miracle drug of the century. Exercise will help you develop a calmer, more relaxed attitude toward daily pressures because of the release of endorphins. Endorphins are small morphine-like chemicals that are secreted in the brain as a result of endurance exercise. Exercise stimulates the body's production of other natural mood elevators as well. Regular exercise is essential for those experiencing mental illness who may be taking medication that can cause weight gain.

Regular exercise makes you feel good. Benefits include an increased sense of accomplishment and well-being; improved sleep; reduced stress, anxiety, and depression; better health; clearer thinking; a stronger immune system; and a leaner body. Choose exercise that you can stick with, something you enjoy doing. Walking, jogging, bicycling, or low-impact aerobics are all good choices, but walking is ideal.

Walking briskly is one of the simplest and best forms of exercise. It's as natural as breathing and has the lowest dropout rate of any form of activity, particularly if you have a compatible walking partner. Walking outdoors gives the added therapeutic benefit of fresh air and sunshine, which can also have a positive affect on your hormonal balance. Walking requires no equipment other than comfortable clothing and well-fitting, supportive shoes. Moderate exercise is ideal, so keep it fun and please don't overdo. Check with your doctor if you have physical limitations. Exercise will lift your spirits, so aim for a twenty- to thirty-minute workout most days of the week. It is a critical factor in achieving the healthiest mind and body possible.

Drink plenty of water before, during if needed, and after exercise to avoid dehydration and to increase your energy level. Pure water is the best liquid you can drink and is vital to good health. Get adequate rest. Learn to rest before you get too tired. A short power nap or a few minutes of total relaxation helps prevent fatigue and keeps you in control.

Take Good Care of Your Body

There is no guarantee that all negative emotions can be solved by taking good care of the physical body, but it is true that body, mind, and spirit are inseparably connected. One does affect the other to a great degree. Stress on the physical body ultimately stresses your emotional well-being. Regular exercise and adequate rest are essential to our lives.

Good Nutrition

How you eat can have a tremendous impact on your emotional health. The reality of this fact was forcefully brought to my attention one morning when I stopped to visit a friend whom I will call Betty. Betty had struggled with a weight and self-esteem problem most of her life due to abuse as a child. She was receiving professional help to cope with chronic depression but had recently started talking of suicide. When Betty invited me in, I could see that a crisis was in the making. She was totally out of control emotionally—crying and distraught. I took her shaking body in my arms and comforted her. She said she'd been skipping meals and then snacking on junk foods, thinking that would help her lose weight for sure. As for exercise, she hadn't been out of the house for days.

Not daring to leave her alone, I took Betty home with me and immediately fixed her some good food. She insisted she wasn't hungry, but like many dieters, anorectics, and others with eating disorders, she was suffering from an artificial suppression of hunger. She didn't feel hungry but was actually starving for good food. Why? The body knows when it isn't getting enough nutrients to meet its nutritional needs, and the metabolism naturally slows down. The individual may feel sick and tired as the body tries to conserve energy. Dieting or eating erratically often triggers a binge later on as the body tries to compensate for nutrients it missed earlier. This type of eating can become a vicious cycle, causing more feelings of sadness and guilt as it drains energy and self-esteem.

Despite her protests, Betty quickly cleaned her plate. Soon after, what seemed to be a miracle took place right before my eyes. Energy and control began to return to her mind and body. She quit shaking and began to think more clearly. Her condition continued to improve through positive conversation, good music, and healthy food. When I took her home after dinner that evening, she was greatly improved. Although Betty continues to receive counseling and is working on her many challenges, this traumatic learning experience regarding the importance of regular, healthy eating was a turning point in her recovery.

"If you want to feel better, start eating better," Karen M. Sunderland and I once wrote. "There is a direct relationship between how you feel and how you eat" (*Set for Life: Eat More, Weigh Less, Feel Terrific!* [Salt Lake City: Sunrise Publishers, 2001], 30).

The Lord's Law of Health

The Lord knew the health challenges we would face today and has given us an iron rod to cling to, the word of God as found in Doctrine and Covenants 89:1–21. Why would the Lord give a revelation that relates to the temporal salvation of his people? The condition of the physical body can affect the spirit, and that is why the Lord gave us the Word of Wisdom. The Word of Wisdom is the most powerful, effective health and weight control program in existence, a true *owner's manual* for the body, whose guidelines will safely guide you through the mass of confusion in the world today regarding the principles of good health. Living the Word of Wisdom induces an internal feeling of calmness and tranquility.

Which foods are best? In Doctrine and Covenants 89:10–17, the Lord identifies the types of foods that are best for the body: all wholesome herbs (plant foods), fresh fruit, and grains, particularly wheat. And he admonishes that meat and fowl be eaten sparingly. Today medical science has proven the validity of following these guidelines to achieve better mental and physical health.

Whole grains, fresh vegetables, and fruit are low-stress, low-calorie, high-fiber, high-energy foods. They are the only category of foods not linked to any long-term health risk. These complex carbohydrates burn cleanly in the body and are the foods the body is designed to run on. They release nutrients slowly into the bloodstream, which provides a long-lasting flow of energy to the body, and they help to regulate blood sugar levels and serotonin production in the brain. "Serotonin is a neurotransmitter that boosts feelings of optimism, well-being, self-esteem, relaxation, and security" (Dr. Joel Robertson, *Natural Prozac* [New York: Harper Collins, 1997], 13). Proper diet and exercise, in conjunction with professional mental health care when needed, play an important role in coping with mental illness or any other illness.

Put the WOW in your life. The Word of Wisdom is for everyone, "adapted to the capacity of the weak and the weakest of all saints, who are or can be called saints" (D&C 89:3). Read and study Doctrine and Covenants 89 and then ask the Lord how it applies to you personally and what you must do to receive these promised blessings: "And all saints who remember to keep and do these sayings, walking in obedience to the commandments, shall receive health in their navel and marrow to their bones; and shall find wisdom and great treasures of knowledge, even hidden treasures; and shall run and not be weary and shall walk and not faint. And I, the Lord, give unto them a promise, that the destroying angel shall pass by them, as the children of Israel, and not slay them" (D&C 89:18–21).

President Gordon B. Hinckley assures us: "Every principle of the gospel carries with it a conviction of its truth, 'if we will prove it.' He told members if they have any question about the Word of Wisdom, to live it and they will come to know it is a true principle of the Almighty given through revelation for the blessing of His children" ("Prophet's Surprise Visit Delights Branch," *Church News,* 21 October 1995, 6).

How you eat plays a significant role in your success! The key is to eat regularly and replace the empty-calorie junk foods in your diet with plenty of satisfying WOW foods. As you change your way of eating, you'll be amazed at how quickly you begin to look and feel better. Learning to eat for how you want to feel is rewarding!

Eat at least three meals a day. Don't skip meals, especially breakfast. Eat wholesome snacks when hungry. Food is fuel, and you can't run on empty very long. Skipping meals often causes dramatic peaks and valleys in your blood sugar and energy levels. When this happens, you are likely to experience negative feelings and behavior, including some types of depression and emotional instability. Going without nourishing food longer than four to five hours may cause you to overeat foods you planned to avoid. When weak, tired, and hungry, you may also find yourself more vulnerable to sin and temptation. Eat at least three good meals a day to fortify and strengthen your body, mind, and spirit. Used wisely, vitamins, minerals and some herbs may also be beneficial.

A nourishing breakfast raises energy and performance levels while also stabilizing emotions. It should help prevent that mid-morning slump that makes many people reach for a sweet snack when their blood sugar plummets. Eating a healthy breakfast will also influence what and how much you eat later in the day. Try starting your day with a low-sugar, high-fiber, whole-grain breakfast such as oatmeal or shredded wheat. Add fruit and a slice or two of whole grain toast if desired. If you are taking medications, make sure there are no restrictions on foods you can eat.

Minimize empty-calorie foods such as white flour products, sugars, soft drinks, diet soda, and artificial sweeteners, and avoid coffee, tea, caffeine, and alcohol. These "foods" can trigger emotional problems because of their effect on blood sugar levels and brain chemistry. And don't let fats and sugars crowd out the beneficial vegetables, fruits, whole grains, and legumes the body needs. You may find that your tastes change as you improve your eating habits and your body lets you know what it needs to be healthy.

Drink eight or more eight-ounce glasses of water daily. Water is perhaps the single most important ingredient in any health program. It increases energy, reduces water retention, flushes out body waste, helps relieve constipation, helps maintain muscle tone, and prevents dehydration.

You don't have to be perfect to be successful! It's natural to have a bad day now and then. When you slip, put that day behind you and don't look back; just begin again. When you're doing things right most of the time, your body is very forgiving. Keep these principles in the back of your mind. Success will come as you take things one day at a time: "By the yard life is hard. By the inch life's a cinch." Change is rewarding as you achieve victory over self. *You can change!* That is the essence of the Savior's message to each of us.

Each has a measure of creation. We have been taught that each of us must reach the measure of our own creation. Now what might the measure of creation be for someone suffering from a form of mental illness? At times one's best effort ends with an individual still having a difficult and challenging life here on earth. For some, even with all the medication, therapy, professional care, and their best personal efforts, the measure of their creation falls short of others' expectations. Don't be discouraged if you are unable to do everything everyone else can do. *But do the best you can.*

Positive living, regular exercise, and good nutrition are an unbeatable combination, and their combined strength will help you *fill the measure of your own creation.* Although there may be some limitations, typically an individual has inherent power to control thoughts, desires, and actions. With God's help, you can do much to improve your emotional and physical strength by working on these three areas. Everyone, including those who suffer from serious disabilities, will benefit from living this lifestyle. Put this simple yet powerful program to the test. Great blessings will come as you do so.

Have the vision to see, the faith to believe, and the courage to do, and you will be successful.

My Testimony

I have a deep and abiding testimony of the truthfulness of the gospel of Jesus Christ. I know that the Lord loves each one of us, that he knows us individually, and that he will bless us as we turn to him for help with our problems and challenges in life. Through personal experience I have learned the value of living the Word of Wisdom, the Lord's law of health, especially the positive elements. You too can gain much from living the principles taught in this revelation from the Lord.

Community Resources for Families

Mark Glade

Mark Glade lives in London, England. He is a licensed clinical social worker and agency director for LDS Family Services. He and his wife, Kyla, have six children. He reviews various family, church, and community resources available to help those coping with mental illness.

Most of us believe that mental illnesses are rare and only happen to someone else. In fact, mental illnesses are common and widespread. Most of us are not prepared to cope with learning that we might have a mental illness or that we might end up caring for a loved one who has a mental illness. Having a mental illness can be physically and emotionally trying and can make us feel vulnerable to the opinions and judgments of others. If you think you or someone you know may have a mental or emotional problem, it is important to remember there is hope and help.

Mental illness affects the sick person, his or her family, his or her friends, his or her fellow Church members, and many others. Individuals close to the person with mental illness who assists in caring for the sick person are typically referred to as caregivers. A caregiver can be a spouse, a friend, a home teacher, a bishop, or any other individual who assists in caring and supporting the person suffering from the mental illness.

It is common for caregivers to experience emotional distress such as denial, guilt, grief, and anger, as well as financial challenges. Yet the caregiver is *not* the one with the mental illness! Caregivers often struggle to understand the causes of the illness and how they can be of help. Caregivers might not know where to go for assistance and feel awkward when they go to places where mental illnesses might be dealt with.

The family structure often changes when caregivers adjust to a person with a mental illness. For example, typically when a child has mental health problems, the parents focus on that child and on the child's problems. Other children may feel left out and neglected and become resentful of the sibling with mental illness. This can lead to even more family stress. Stress of a chronic and persistent mental illness often leads to disagreements among caregivers. Caregivers may blame each other for what has happened, or they may totally disagree about the treatment plan for the person suffering.

In most cases caregivers have not caused the emotional problem. Although some life stressors may trigger a mental illness, mental health problems usually result from a chemical imbalance. Nevertheless, if you are suffering from a mental illness, you are responsible for managing your life—including your mental illness—the best you can. If you are a caregiver, then you are responsible to help and care for the person suffering in a Christlike fashion.

Develop a Personal Support System

Perhaps the single most important step in surviving mental illness is for you to develop a support system. Most mental illnesses can last a lifetime, with highs and lows periodically occurring. Alone, this path can be devastating and overwhelming. Building a personal support system is essential for both those who are suffering from a mental illness and those who are caregivers. Select members for your support system from those persons you have easy access to. With the advent of the Internet, that could be just about anybody, anywhere.

Nonprofessional Support System

A support system usually includes health care professionals and such nonprofessionals as family members, Church members, and friends.

Family Members

The family can be one of the most important and lasting resources you have. The family already has an existing structure and mode of operation. These processes can be immediately put into place to assist a family member who suffers from a mental illness.

Family council and family home evening. Family gatherings are ideal settings to consider the nature and extent of the illness. It is a time to share and develop plans for assistance. The family needs to become educated about the illness. Literature and resource material can be shared. It may be an opportunity to invite professionals to meet with the family to explain the disorder and to provide professional guidance as to treatment and care. Families may determine roles each family member can play in assisting. These roles will prevent confusion and frustration as time goes on. The spiritual aspects of support such as prayer, fasting, blessings, and special temple sessions can be discussed. Financial aspects of the illness may need to be considered, as mental illnesses often require hospitalization and extensive follow-up.

Finally, family members may need a forum to share their feelings and grieve over a loss. This sometimes can be overlooked, but it is essential as family members adjust to the changes created within the home. Grieving is a process and needs to be recognized as normal and ongoing. Each individual will adapt uniquely to the change, and allowances needed to be made for these alterations.

Family networking. As time passes, other family members will need to be informed of the illness. This is especially true when the family members live apart. A central information-clearing place needs to be established where information is gathered and transmitted. This will prevent misunderstandings and miscommunication.

Family gatherings. Preparation will assist in creating a positive experience for all. Family members need to prepare themselves and others to assist those who may be ill and to prepare those extended family members who may be less aware of the difficulties. Education is the most important factor.

Church Members

Local Church leaders can be of great assistance in offering temporary relief and support for a family living with a mentally ill person. The nature and extent of the mental illness will require local adaptation of the following suggestions.

Provide respite assistance for the main caregivers. Arrange to have a ward member or members spend time with the individual who has the mental illness. Providing this type of assistance can allow the family to renew themselves. Evidence suggests the care of the chronically ill can create emotional hardships on the caregiver.

Spiritual questions. Bishops and other leaders offer a spiritual reservoir to answer the questions and concerns of family members. Often, the caregivers will need blessings.

As is appropriate, consider special fasts, temple blessings, ward council meetings, and welfare meetings to discuss the special needs of the designated family. Consider specialists in the ward or stake who may provide support and assistance to the family. The Lord's storehouse system includes all ward members.

Friends

Friends and associates need to be educated and informed about the nature of the illness. The information that you share will vary based on the extent friends are involved with your family. When sharing information, consider the needs of the individual afflicted with the illness. Inappropriate sharing of information may cause embarrassment or hurt to the individual suffering.

Friends vary. Do not hesitate to set appropriate boundaries. Be comfortable with what you need to share as distinct from what you could share.

Do not expect friends to do that which you can do for yourself or that which your family can do.

Sometimes a friend can be a good and safe "sounding board" when difficulties arise. Know when and with whom to share.

Working with Your Nonprofessional Support System

The following are some suggestions that might help your selected family member, Church member, or friend in becoming a more effective support system.

Keep selected members of your support system informed. A friend, family, or Church member can assist in many ways. Not everyone in your support system will know everything about your struggles.

Educate your support system. Perhaps one of the most challenging tasks in dealing with mental illness is education. Usually there are two areas in which education is required. The first is in working through the denial and accepting that you or someone you care for truly has a mental illness. The second area is in reducing the stigma associated with having a mental illness. A variety of resources in books, articles, and Internet sites are now available to assist in these tasks.

Have at least one member of your support system monitor your spiritual progress. Because most often your professional health care providers will not be active members of the LDS Church, identify someone close to you to assist you in staying close to the Lord and the gospel. Perhaps a periodic interview with your bishop or branch president may assist in evaluating the treatment you are receiving.

Keep learning. New information about mental illness is rapidly forthcoming. Make it a goal to keep learning. Many books and pamphlets are available. For example, several authors in this book have written complete books on their respective topics. Emma Lou Thayne and her daughter have written *Hope and Recovery: A Mother-Daughter Story about Anorexia Nervosa, Bulimia, and Manic Depression* about their personal story. The website located at mentalhealthlibrary.info can also serve as an excellent source of information.

Professional Support System

In addition to friends, family, and fellow Church members, those with mental illness will likely need health care professionals. Ideally, it would be best to have access to a range of mental health professionals including social workers, psychologists, and psychiatrists. In addition, it would be wonderful if each was an active member of the LDS Church, but that usually is not the case. Often your health care system determines who you can see and who you cannot see.

In countries that have a national health care system, there may be little choice of who provides the actual professional care, although private consultations can be made. Many national health care systems use a three-tier approach beginning with the primary physician (GP). The GP will make a decision relating to the extent of intervention needed. If a referral is made, it will be to a counselor or a psychologist. If more extensive assistance is necessary, a referral to a medical specialist such as a psychiatrist will be made. The following are some suggestions that might help your therapist or counselor and/or prescriber of medicine to be a more effective member of your support system.

Try to keep a good personal record. List names, addresses, phone numbers, dates of crisis, admissions to hospitals, administered medications, dosage of medication, and dates of discharge. Make notes when possible of conversations and conferences with your health care providers. Make copies of everything you mail. Keep all notices and letters. (Caution: with some types of mental health problems, such as an obsessive-compulsive disorder, record keeping may be counterproductive).

Inform your health care provider of any significant changes. Make sure you tell the health care worker about side effects of medications and results of any treatment interventions. Side effects are the physical, emotional or mental effects of medication not related to the defined problems. If suicide has been a concern, caregivers must be particularly cautious in monitoring self-harm tendencies and reporting problems immediately.

Do your best in following instructions. Don't miss appointments. Attend the required meetings. It there are homework assignments, do them. If medications are involved, take the medicine exactly as prescribed.

Ask questions. It is best to ask questions before and while you are receiving professional health care. If there is something you do not understand, ask for clarification. Ask about where you can learn more. Know what your diagnosis is and what it means. If the health care provider is too busy to answer your question, find another source. Often another support staff member, such as a nurse or pharmacist, can be of assistance.

We would like to assume that every health care provider is of high quality and ethical; however, we live in an imperfect world, and obtaining a suitable therapist or counselor can at times be difficult. If you are confronted with a provider who doesn't seem to be helping or is encouraging you to violate your personal values and religious beliefs, ask for a new provider. At times, a health care provider may suggest you engage in some behavior or change your values to do something contrary to the teaching of the Church. In such cases, rely on other members of your support system who understand and accept your belief system. Be cautious about mental health interventions that guarantee change.

What about self-help/support groups? Another excellent source of support can be various support groups. Self-help support groups bring together people with common experiences. Participants share experiences, provide understanding and support, and help each other find new ways to cope with problems. Support groups exist for almost any concern, including alcoholism, the loss of a child, codependency, overeating, various mental illnesses, cancer, parenting issues, and many others. Perhaps the best known of such groups is Alcoholics Anonymous (AA).

There are advantages and disadvantages of support groups. Advantages include the following:

- No charge

- Literature is often available

- Typically you can find someone with your mental health concern who has progressed further than you that you can learn from.

Disadvantages include the following:

- Groups moderated by nonprofessionals

- Encouragement to disclose unnecessary personal information

- Leading members away from religious teachings

- Groups that become dysfunctional

With increased access to the Internet, support groups, bulletin boards or chat rooms, nearly any type of mental health concern can now be easily located electronically.

Use good judgment if you decide to participate in a support group. A good rule of thumb is *do not become over reliant on a support group* for your primary source of support. Usually support groups provide services for both the person who is experiencing the mental health issue as well as caregivers who live with them.

Am I Getting the Care I Need?

Periodically ask yourself, "Am I getting the care I need?" If you are a caregiver, ask, "Is my loved one getting the care he or she needs?" Evaluate your support system and more particularly the health care services. As you or your loved one progresses through the recovery process, improvements should usually occur. The person suffering from the mental illness should experience a gradual relief from distress, an increase in self-assurance, a greater ability to make decisions, and increased comfort in his or her relationship with others.

Therapy may be painful and uncomfortable at times, but episodes of discomfort occur during the most successful therapy sessions. In any illness, there is a period of convalescence. There may be relapses and times of tension and resentment. Mental health treatment should help you cope with your feelings more effectively. If you feel you are not getting results, it may be because the treatment you are receiving is not the one best suited to your specific needs. If you feel there are problems, discuss them with your health care provider. A competent therapist will be eager to discuss your reactions to therapy and respond to your feeling about the process. If you are still dissatisfied, a consultation with another therapist may help you and your therapist evaluate your work together. It is important to remember that there is hope for recovery and that with treatment many people with mental illness return to a productive and fulfilling life; however, do not expect an immediate, 100 percent recovery.

A Word of Caution for Caregivers

It is common for the person with the mental illness to become the focus of family life. When this happens, other members of the family may feel ignored or resentful. As a caregiver, you may find it hard to pursue your own interests, including spiritual interests. If you are the caregiver, *you* need some time for yourself. Schedule time away *to prevent* your becoming frustrated or angry. Scheduling time for yourself will help you to keep things in perspective, and you may have more patience and compassion for coping or helping your loved one. Only when you are physically and emotionally healthy can you help others.

Trust in the Lord

Although finding resources to adequately deal with a mental illness can be difficult, it is still your responsibility to do so. It's not unusual to take several months to locate a proper mental health care provider and, if medication is required, several more months before an effective combination of medication can be found. Don't be discouraged. Use your support system and rely on the Lord the best you can. Do your best to continue regular church attendance, scripture study, and personal prayer.

Elder Richard G. Scott has given us some excellent advice:

> Oh, how we all need the healing the Redeemer can provide. Mine is a message of hope for you who yearn for relief from heavy burdens that have come through no conscious act of your own while you have lived a worthy life. It is based on the principles embodied in the teachings of the Savior. Your challenge may be a serious physical disability, a struggle with lingering illness, or a daily wrestle with a life-threatening disease. It may have roots in the death of a loved one, the anguish caused by another bound by sin, or come from abuse in any of its evil forms. Whatever the cause I testify that lasting relief is available on conditions established by the Lord. . . .
>
> Recognize that some challenges in life will not be resolved here on earth. . . . [The Lord] wants you to learn how to be cured when that is His will and how to obtain strength to live with your challenge when He intends it to be an instrument for growth. In either case the Redeemer will support you. . . .
>
> Don't say, "No one understands me; I can't sort it out, or get the help I need." Those comments are self-defeating. No one can help you without faith and effort on your part. Your personal growth requires that. Don't look for a life virtually free from discomfort, pain, pressure, challenge, or grief, for those are the tools a loving Father uses to stimulate

our personal growth and understanding. . . . Your access to the Savior's help comes in different ways. The most direct and often the most powerful way is through humble, trusting prayers to your Father in Heaven, which are answered through the Holy Ghost to your spirit. . . .

Even if they had unlimited time and resources, which they don't, priesthood leaders could not provide all of the help. They are agents of the Lord, and His law requires that you do your part. They will show you the way. They can provide priesthood blessings. Your faith, purity, and obedience and that of the priesthood holder have great effect on the pronouncement and realization of the blessing. Healing can occur in the act, yet more often it occurs over a period of time determined by the faith and obedience of the individual and the will of the Lord. I feel the pace is generally set by the individual and not by the Lord. *He expects you to use other resources available, including competent professional help when indicated. . . .*

Yet, no matter what the source of difficulty and no matter how you begin to obtain relief—through a qualified professional therapist, doctor, priesthood leader, friend, concerned parent, or loved one—no matter how you begin, those solutions will never provide a complete answer. The final healing comes through faith in Jesus Christ and His teachings, with a broken heart and a contrite spirit and obedience to His commandments. ("To Be Healed," *Ensign,* May 1994, 7; emphasis added)

Trials and tribulations are not unfamiliar to the Latter-day Saints. The Lord said, "And we will prove them herewith, to see if they will do all things whatsoever the Lord their God shall command them" (Abraham 3:25). The natural part of us would like to avoid all these challenges, the better part of us wants to select what problems we experience, but the most noble part of us accepts whatever "afflicts" us and works in humility to find answers.

It is my testimony that answers come to each of us. Often they come through other people and avenues that we had never considered. The most wonderful gift that can come to us is the sweet whisperings of the Spirit that enlarge our souls and enlighten our minds. Through his grace we will experience hope "and the peace of God, which passeth all understanding" (Philippians 4:7). When we submit our wills to that of the Father, we begin to heal and life refreshes us again.

Caring and Helping

C. Max Caldwell

Elder C. Max Caldwell served as a member of the Second Quorum of the Seventy from 1992 to 1997. He and his wife, Joann, are the parents of five children.

As we speak of the role of Church members and leaders in connection with mental health education, I believe all of us feel we are on an exciting threshold of acquiring and developing new insights. For many of us, this is a new frontier, yet to be explored. Though some may have had extensive exposure and involvement, many others have had precious little or even no awareness of the issues at hand and the real needs of some of our brothers and sisters. All of us, regardless of our background, can improve our usefulness by increasing our knowledge and furthering our involvement.

The Lord has called and placed each of you in key positions so that he might utilize your talents and capabilities for the benefit of his children. Who knows but that a major purpose or reason for your present Church assignment might be that you could be the means, in his hands, of opening doors of healing and relief for someone currently suffering from some form of mental illness? And that someone may not even know or understand his own condition, yet be a needy and worthy citizen of Father's kingdom within the reach of your stewardship service opportunities.

In our relationship responsibilities with each other, our roles might be described as two dimensional with a one-word definition of each: *caring* and *helping*.

Caring

I believe that caring about people as individuals is not only a desirable and enviable component of our nature but also a prerequisite character trait that determines the quantity and quality of assistance we might render to others. Only when people care will they help.

From the pen of Marjorie Spiller Neagle comes one of my favorite accounts of a true-life experience:

> "When I was young, and pretty much satisfied with myself," an elderly man once told me, "I spent a college vacation looking for what I called 'local color' for use in a book I planned to write. My main character was to be drawn from an impoverished, shiftless community, and I believed I knew just where to find it.
>
> "Sure enough, one day I came upon the place, made to order with its rundown farms, seedy men and washed-out women. To top it off, the epitome of the shiftlessness I had envisioned was waiting for me near an unpainted shack, in the shape of a scraggly-bearded old man in faded overalls who was hoeing around a little patch of potatoes while sitting in a chair.
>
> "I started back to my rooming house, itching to get at my typewriter. As I made the turn in the dirt road which ran past the cabin, I looked at the scene from another angle. And when I did, I saw something which stopped me cold in my tracks. For from this side, I observed, leaning against the chair, a pair of crutches, and I noticed one empty overall leg hanging limply to the ground. In that instant the lazy, shiftless character I had seen was transformed into a figure of dauntless courage."
>
> Since that hour I have never judged a man after only one look or one conversation with him. And I thank God that I turned for the second look. ("The Peerless Potentate of Pachydermia," *Reader's Digest*, November 1971, 137)

Properly perceiving people makes possible the development of a caring attitude within us. The so-called lazy potato-hoeing man was not transformed; he didn't change at all. The change occurred in the eye and heart of the beholder. Instead of seeing a shiftless character, he ultimately saw a person admirably coping with physical limitations and doing what he could to lead and live a productive life. The writer's judgment of the man's values and needs changed as he acquired an awareness of the disability that dictated and determined behavior patterns. The second look provided the writer with a new vision of reality that already existed for the bearded old man in faded overalls. And that new view created new feelings of compassion, admiration, and respect for the nobility of a fellow human being. New feelings of caring were conceived.

We should be reminded of the Savior's declaration that "the worth of souls is great *in the sight of God*" (D&C 8:10; emphasis added). The Lord's view never needs to be enhanced by a second look. It seems that our need is to seek to acquire his perspective and look upon the souls of God's sons and daughters rather than risk rendering inaccurate judgments based upon limited and faulty views of outward appearances or actions. Appropriate and adequate assistance depends upon accurate assessments. No one in Church leadership positions can afford to rely on personal wisdom without the directing and confirming influence of the Holy Spirit. Like Nephi, we need to be "led by the Spirit, not knowing beforehand the things which [we] should do" (1 Nephi 4:6).

In the situation just described, the subject was a man with physical disabilities. But what of individuals who live with both internal and external consequences of mental illness? They may or may not exhibit a physical or outward manifestation of their inward conditions. Their suffering may never be seen through observations of physical situations only. But their afflicted souls need the caring concern of the Lord's people who are already committed to a covenant of "bear[ing] one another's burdens, that they may be light; yea, and are willing to mourn with those that mourn; yea, and comfort those that stand in need of comfort" (Mosiah 18:8–9). Perhaps our compassion would be enhanced if we better understood the feelings of the sufferer.

Let me read to you one of King David's psalms. Would you wonder with me if he might have been inspired to write a prayer that could also be heard as a reflection of the passionate pleadings of a soul plagued with mental illness? Such people typically feel terribly alone among their mortal associates. Often, in desperation, they cry unto the Lord, seeking relief and freedom from imprisoned feelings. As you listen, take special note of a statement that might be considered to be the saddest statement in all holy writ:

> I cried unto the Lord with my voice; with my voice unto the Lord did I make my supplication. I poured out my complaint before him; I shewed before him my trouble. When my spirit was overwhelmed within me, then thou knewest my path. In the way wherein I walked have they privily laid a snare for me. I looked on my right hand, and beheld, but there was no man that would know me: refuge failed me; *no man cared for my soul.* I cried unto thee, O Lord: I said, Thou art my refuge and my portion in the land of the living. Attend unto my cry; for I am brought very low: deliver me from my persecutors; for they are stronger than I. Bring my soul out of prison, that I may praise thy name: the righteous shall compass me about; for thou shalt deal bountifully with me. (Psalm 142:1–7; emphasis added)

I think we must never, never, never permit any human being within our circle of influence to think no one cares for his or her soul. Not only must we be obedient to the Lord's second commandment and love our neighbor but we must also be certain those feelings are not wrapped in a shroud of secrecy. If our neighbor doesn't know of our love, it is the same to him as if such feelings don't exist. Our love cannot be conditional or dependent upon our convenience or preconceived notions; nor can it depend upon our perception of the behavior, attitude, or even illness of others. Sometimes the most unlovable are those who need love the most. Consider the Savior's experience with the rich young man, as recorded by Mark:

> And when [Jesus] was gone forth into the way, there came one running, and kneeled to him, and asked him, Good Master, what shall I do that I may inherit eternal life? And Jesus said unto him, . . . Thou knowest the commandments, do not commit

adultery, do not kill, do not steal, do not bear false witness, defraud not, honour thy father and mother. And he answered and said unto him, Master, all these have I observed from my youth. Then Jesus *beholding him loved him,* and said unto him, One thing thou lackest. (Mark 10:17–21; emphasis added)

Jesus then proceeded to give him direction that, if heeded, would eliminate the problem or condition wherein he was lacking. We take note of two things from this encounter.

First, Jesus' response and counsel to the young man was based upon having first "beheld" him. Jesus clearly saw his soul, observed his need, and specifically declared him to be lacking in at least one thing.

Second, though the young man was lacking, though he might have had an undesirable problem, though he might have been demonstrating an offensive nature, though his actions and attitude might even have been distasteful to the sensitive nature of him who beheld, still the scripture records that Jesus "loved him." I am impressed that our Savior would look upon a man, who, like me, may have many problems, weaknesses, or afflictions, and yet beholding him, "loved him."

And so it is with us. In our encounters with others, we must seek to behold the real strength and value of souls without waiting or hoping for a second look that may not be possible and may never occur. We need to discover, as accurately as possible, what condition of weakness prevails, or in other words, in what way a person is "lacking." It may be mental, physical, emotional, or spiritual. But it needs to be identified. In the case of many mental afflictions, it is well to remember that neither the individual nor his family has usually done anything to cause the illness with its attendant difficult-to-understand behavior. Furthermore, the person so afflicted is typically not empowered with the ability to overcome the illness and lift himself out of the depths of despair and depression. The illness is usually a "no-fault" condition with an attached "no-fix" solution. So we remember the worth of souls—and we care.

Furthermore, there should be an awareness on our part and in the hearts of others that we love regardless of what people may lack. No one should have reason to believe that no one cares. Though the individual may be figuratively or even literally "far away," we must do as did the prodigal's father who, when he saw his lacking son "a great way off," yet had "compassion" for him and, beholding him, hurried to fill his needs and assure him of his love (Luke 15:20).

Helping

The second topic is *helping*. To set the stage for our discussion, may I again turn to the scripture and read a few verses:

> And as Jesus passed by, he *saw* a man which was blind from his birth. And his disciples asked him, saying, Master, who did sin, this man, or his parents, that he was born blind? Jesus answered, *Neither hath this man sinned, nor his parents*: but that the works of God should be made manifest in him. (John 9:1–3; emphasis added)

Neither the man nor his family was responsible for his ailment. Jesus healed the man of his blindness, and the Jews challenged the source of the power by which the blindness was removed and sight bestowed. The healed man defended Jesus by saying, "If this man [Jesus] were not of God, he could do nothing" (John 9:33). Let's review the sequence. After Jesus truly "saw" or "beheld" the blind man, He determined that help could be extended and proceeded to remove the affliction. Now there is a principle to be learned.

Sometimes God is willing, without assistance, to perform a work in behalf of those who may be lacking. But his help commonly comes through the involvement of people who are willing to help others under the direction and by the approval of the Almighty. The performance of the works of God depends upon the faithful and diligent service of the servants of God. And how are the servants to assist in the recovery process for those who are afflicted with mental illness?

There is an order to things in the Lord's kingdom. Again we turn to the scriptures, where we are told that "it is by grace that we are saved, *after all we can do*" (2 Nephi 25:23; emphasis added). In other words, we can expect the Lord's blessings will be bestowed after we have done all we can within our limited knowledge and ability. We ought not to expect the Lord to perform a healing or adjust degrees of suffering until we have used our currently existing resources and accomplished whatever we have the capability to do. The Lord has revealed many ways mankind can help themselves and prevent or obtain relief from many illnesses and diseases. In addition to calling on the Lord for divine intervention, we are expected to utilize the knowledge and skills of those endowed with the ability to provide counsel and treatment in our afflictions. Many medical processes, procedures, and substances have been revealed through the light of Christ to the scientific community in these latter days. Our responsibility to use these resources was explained by President Brigham Young when he taught the following:

> You may go to some people here, and ask what ails them, and they answer, 'I don't know, but we feel a dreadful distress in the stomach and in the back; we feel all out of order, and we wish you to lay hands upon us.' 'Have you used any remedies?' 'No. We wish the Elders to lay hands upon us, and we have faith that we shall be healed.' That is inconsistent according to my faith. If we are sick, and ask the Lord to heal us, and to do all for us that is necessary to be done, according to my understanding of the Gospel of salvation, I might as well ask the Lord to cause my wheat and corn to grow, without my plowing the ground and casting in the seed. It appears consistent to me to apply every remedy that comes within the range of my knowledge, and to ask my Father in heaven, in the name of Jesus Christ, to sanctify that application to the healing of my body; to another this may appear inconsistent.
>
> But supposing we were traveling in the mountains, and all we had or could get, in the shape of nourishment, was a little venison, and one or two were taken sick, without anything in the world in the shape of healing medicine within our reach, what should we do? According to my faith, ask the Lord Almighty to send an angel to heal the sick. This is our privilege, when so situated that we cannot get

anything to help ourselves. Then the Lord and his servants can do all. But it is my duty to do, when I have it in my power. Many people are unwilling to do one thing for themselves in case of sickness but ask God to do it all (in *Journal of Discourses*, 26 vols. [London: Latter-day Saints' Book Depot, 1854–86], 4:24–25)

We have already determined that Church leaders must first care for the afflicted and be filled with love for them so that when they behold they might also accurately discern individual needs. This ability is developed in part as church leaders seek to learn about and recognize symptoms that reveal inward needs. They must also be informed of sources of professional expertise which can provide immeasurable help to those afflicted with an illness they cannot cure themselves. This is the value of mental health education. (The preceding chapters provide education.)

As an example of this process, let me share with you something personal. Members of my own family have experienced various anxiety and depressive symptoms of mental illness. For some time, I was unaware of what was happening and at a loss to determine any course of action that might provide relief for them. Though I loved them, sympathized with them, and cared terribly that they were suffering, I was blind to the problem, and the people with whom I talked offered no help. I prayed intensely and incessantly for my loved ones' relief but to no avail. Priesthood blessings offered hope, but it didn't come right then. I wondered when and how any help might be found. One day I received a telephone call from a family member who had, that very day, attended a medical symposium and heard discussions of these problems, including the typical symptoms associated with it. Everything fit our situation. So we obtained the services of a medical specialist who had acquired a great deal of expertise in the field. We found and used available resources that provided help and relief and a return to a more normal lifestyle for our family. The blessing came only as we did all we could do, including the involvement of another family member who cared and was inspired to help us find solutions to some difficult problems. Recognizing the condition and knowing where to turn for help were key to the resolving process.

The Lord has directed that Church leaders should magnify their callings, whatever they may be. The word "magnify" may be understood to mean "enlarge." In order for an enlargement to take place, one needs to gather the powers of the existing resources and focus them on a given point. This is illustrated in the process by which a magnifying lens enlarges by focusing the powers of available light. Church leaders can be measurably more helpful and effective when they become informed of the problems associated with mental illness with their accompanying symptoms and potential solutions. Only then will they be able to magnify their calling by use of available information and resources, thus being enabled to provide appropriate assistance to those who live within the circle of their personal association and ecclesiastical responsibility.

Without sufficient sensitivity to mental illness symptoms, Church leaders could mistakenly interpret a person's unacceptable outward behavior as an attitude problem and take up a labor of counseling to persuade the individual to make personality and attitude changes. Sometimes, Church leaders have told victims of mental illness that if they would be more faithful in their prayers and scripture study, they would grow stronger in the Spirit and thus be able to lift themselves out of their depressive conditions. Unwittingly, some have even said, "I know you can do it if you work at it hard enough." Though the counsel and challenging encouragement is well-intentioned and could surely be expected to provide for personal spiritual growth and motivation, still, the illness is not likely to change by simply following that course only. Instead, the victim of the illness will likely try to please Church leaders, family, and friends, and when conditions don't improve, feel an even greater sense of frustration and failure than before.

The helping influence we offer needs to be based on the qualities and conditions outlined by the Lord, when he said: "No power or influence can or ought to be maintained by virtue of the priesthood, only by persuasion, by long-suffering, by gentleness and meekness, and by *love unfeigned;* by kindness, and *pure knowledge*" (D&C 121:41–42; emphasis added).

The clergy and membership of the Lord's Church can be effective in ministering to those with mental illness by functioning in two specific ways. First, we need to care by having charity, the pure love of Christ. Second, we need to help by providing appropriate counseling and guidance in using available resources, especially in seeking and obtaining heavenly powers.

May each of us merit the praise, gratitude, and blessings Joseph Smith extended to his beloved brother Hyrum, when he said:

> Brother Hyrum, what a faithful heart you have got! Oh may the Eternal Jehovah crown eternal blessings upon your head, as a reward for *the care you have had for my soul!* O how many are the sorrows we have shared together; and again we find ourselves shackled with the unrelenting hand of oppression. Hyrum, thy name shall be written in the book of the law of the Lord, for those who come after thee to look upon, that they may pattern after thy works. (*History of The Church of Jesus Christ of Latter-day Saints,* ed. B. H. Roberts, 2d ed. rev., 7 vols. [Salt Lake City: The Church of Jesus Christ of Latter-day Saints, 1932–51], 5:107–8; emphasis added)

May we seek the Lord's vision of values and his divine direction as we search for the most suitable means of healing the afflicted so that we might fulfill and honor our sacred trust in behalf of Father's sons and daughters. I know he cares and provides help for all who seek it from him. He lives. He is our God. This I know and declare as a witness of him.

This chapter comes from a presentation given during conferences of the Cache Valley chapter of the National Alliance for the Mentally Ill in North Logan, Utah, October 28, 2000, and in Richmond, Utah, April 28, 2001.

Resource Listings

Mental Health Resource Foundation

The Foundation's Interests

The Mental Health Resource Foundation is a private, nonprofit foundation incorporated in 1991. The Foundation's interests are to identify, develop, and promote resources for persons with mental health concerns. Mental health concerns include mental illnesses such as depression, bipolar, schizophrenia, anxiety, and eating disorders; and social/emotional concerns including alcohol and drug abuse, same-sex attraction, pornography, divorce, and physical and sexual abuse.

Position on Mental Illness

The Foundation believes that mental illness is a brain disorder. "It is an illness that affects or is manifested in a person's brain. It may impact on the way a person thinks, behaves, and interacts with other people . . . Mental illnesses are real illnesses—as real as heart disease and cancer" (American Psychiatric Association) The foundation recognizes that mental and physical diseases are much alike. We agree with the National Alliance of the Mentally Ill (NAMI) that "mental illnesses are not the result of personal weakness, lack of character, or poor upbringing. Mental illnesses are treatable."

Position on Other Social and Emotional Concerns

The Foundation believes that there are social/emotional concerns that result from environment, experiences, and choices. Societal issues such as alcohol and drug abuse, same-sex attraction, pornography, divorce, and physical and sexual abuse can profoundly disrupt a person's capacity for coping with the demands of life. The

Foundation acknowledges that people with serious social/emotional concerns can, with proper education and assistance, attain their highest level of productivity.

The Problem

There is an epidemic of mental, social, and emotional problems. Members of various religions rely on their respective beliefs and religious leaders for guidance in their personal lives regarding mental illness and social/emotional concerns. The religious community's challenge of dealing with mental health issues, often lacking faith-based resources, is enormous. Faith leaders and their members have an ongoing need for easily accessible and useful mental health resources as well as practical guides for using such resources.

The Solution

The solution is twofold. First, identify and develop useful resources. Second, make these resources available to those in need. In addition to appropriate professional care, the Foundation believes that quality of life for those with mental health concerns can be significantly improved by increasing spirituality, improving family relations, developing an effective support system, and seeking knowledge. The Foundation's mission is to reduce the burden of mental health concerns through resource development, education, and providing resources that strengthen the individual and the family.

The Foundation continues to

- Develop a faith-based Internet library on a range of mental illnesses including depression, bipolar disorder, schizophrenia, anxiety, and eating disorders. Resources on social/emotional concerns such as alcohol and drug abuse, same-sex attraction, pornography, divorce, and physical and sexual abuse are also available.

- Educate religious communities concerning mental illness and social/emotional issues to increase understanding, improve attitudes, and reduce stigmas.

- Provide resources that include electronic and printed materials to help families, churches, organizations, and professional caregivers.

- Strengthen the individual's and the family's spiritual foundation.

Websites

Mental Health Library
Mental Health Resource Foundation
2550 Washington Blvd. Suite 103
P.O. Box 3074
Ogden, Utah 84409
(801) 621–8484 or (800) 723–1760
Website: http://mentalhealthlibrary.info
E-mail: Info@MentalHealthLibrary.info

National Institute of Mental Health (NIMH)
Office of Communications
6001 Executive Boulevard, Room 8184, MSC 9663
Bethesda, MD 20892–9663
Phone: 301–443–4513 or 1–866–615-NIMH (6464), toll-free
TTY: 301–443–8431; FAX: 301–443–4279
FAX 4U: 301–443–5158
Website: http://www.nimh.nih.gov
E-mail: nimhinfo@nih.gov

National Alliance for the Mentally Ill (NAMI)
Colonial Place Three
2107 Wilson Blvd., Suite 300
Arlington, VA 22201–3042
1–800–950-NAMI (6264)
TDD: (703) 516–7227
Website: http:// www.nami.org
E-mail: campaign@nami.org

Useful Books

Merrill, Jane P., and Karen M. Sunderland. "*Boarding the Ark Today: Featuring Hundreds of Tasty Recipes for the 21st Century.*" Salt Lake City: Sunrise Publishers, 1999.

———. *Set for Life: Eat More, Weigh Less, Feel Terrific!* Salt Lake City: Sunrise Publishers, 2001.

Morrison, Alexander B. *Valley of Sorrow: A Layman's Guide to Understanding Mental Illness.* Salt Lake City: Deseret Book, 2003.

Thayne, Emma Lou, and Becky Thayne Markosian. *Hope and Recovery: A Mother-Daughter Story about Anorexia Nervosa, Bulimia, and Manic Depression.* New York: Franklin Watts, 1992.